Christian Basics

Lessons, Debates, and Conversations

Kent Philpott

EVP

Earthen Vessel Publishing
San Rafael, CA

Christian Basics
Lessons, Debates, and Conversations

All rights reserved
Copyright © 2015 by Kent A. Philpott

Published 2015 by Earthen Vessel Publishing
San Rafael, CA 94903
www.evpbooks.com

Revised first edition ISBN: 978-0-9907277-8-1
(First edition ISBN: 978-0-9907277-2-9)

Library of Congress Control Number: 2015931489

Cover and Book Design by Katie L. C. Philpott

No part of this publication may be reproduced, stored in a retrieval system, or transmitted in any form or by any means, electronic or mechanical, including photocopying, recording, or by any information retrieval system, without the written permission of the author or publisher, except by a reviewer who wishes to quote brief passages in connection with a review written for inclusion in a magazine, newspaper, internet site, or broadcast.

All Scripture quotations, unless otherwise indicated, are taken from the Holy Bible, English Standard Version® (ESV®), copyright © 2001 by Crossway Bibles, a publishing ministry of Good News Publishers. Used by permission. All rights reserved.

Dedicated to all who seek the truths of God

Contents

Book Introduction ... 1
The Basic Lessons
  The God Who Reveals Himself
    The God of the Bible ... 6
    Revelation ... 9
    Scripture ... 12
    The Old Testament ... 15
    The New Testament ... 19
    How We Got the Bible ... 24
    The Great Paradoxes of the Bible ... 28
  The Great Themes of the Bible
    Election ... 34
    Presence ... 39
    Rest ... 43
    Peace ... 47
    Two Messiahs ... 50
    Judgment ... 54
    Persecution/Triumph of Christ's Church ... 60
  The Church and Christian Life
    The Church ... 68
    The Christian Ethic ... 74
    The Christian Life ... 78
    Church History ... 85

Debates and Conversations
  Extramural Debates
    Extramural Debates: Introduction   *90*
    The Exclusivity of Jesus   *92*
    The Authority of Scripture   *94*
    Heaven *and* Hell   *97*
    Same-Sex Marriage   *99*
  Intramural Conversations
    Intramural Conversations: Introduction   *106*
    Abortion   *107*
    Baptism and The Lord's Supper   *109*
    Church Government   *112*
    Divorce and Remarriage   *117*
    Ecumenism   *120*
    End Times   *122*
    Gifts of the Holy Spirit   *126*
    Music in the Church   *129*
    Origins   *132*
    Politics and War   *135*
    Reformed vs. Arminian Theologies   *137*
    Women in the Church   *140*

Final Note   *143*
Other Books by Kent Philpott   *144*

Book Introduction

As Christians we are "disciples," which means we learn from the Master. Part of this involves learning who God is, reading what Jesus taught and did, and discovering the doctrines that we see in the Scripture. Jesus instructed His followers, "Go therefore and make disciples of all nations, baptizing them in the name of the Father and of the Son and of the Holy Spirit, teaching them to observe all that I have commanded you" (Matthew 28:19–20).

God has provided means for this learning to be accomplished and the reasons why it is so important. We find this in Ephesians 4:11–14:

> And he gave the apostles, the prophets, the evangelists, the pastors and teachers, to equip the saints for the work of ministry, for building up of the body of Christ, until we all attain to the unity of the faith and of the knowledge of the Son of God, to mature manhood, to the measure of the stature of the fullness of Christ, so that we may no longer be children, tossed to and fro by

the waves and carried about by every wind of doctrine, by human cunning, by craftiness in deceitful schemes.

This learning is a lifelong process and is part of the joy of being a follower of Jesus. It all begins with the new birth. As there is a physical maturation process that extends from infancy to our death, so there is a similar spiritual process. We approach it little by little, but it must be deliberate and focused. There is a reason why the Church through the ages has maintained schools where new Christians are taught the richness of their theologies.

Christian Basics is just that; it is where we start, where we lay down a foundation upon which to build. Paul wrote these words to his disciple Timothy: "Do your best to present yourself to God as one approved, a worker who has no need to be ashamed, rightly handling the word of truth" (2 Timothy 2:15).

Section One comprises the Christian Basics, divided into three parts. Part One is entitled "The God Who Reveals Himself" and consists of seven lessons that form the foundation for Part Two, "The Great Themes of the Bible," which consists of five lessons that describe central biblical themes. Part Three, "The Church and the Christian Life," contains four lessons.

Section Two, is entitled "Extramural Debates and Intramural Conversations." The four debates are those doctrines that are central to Christianity and without which there is no essential and biblical Christianity. The twelve conversations consider issues that Christians often disagree upon, sometimes hotly.

No two Christians agree on everything, yet all Christians agree on key doctrines, the points of which are summarized in the Apostles' Creed. It is, in fact, healthy that Christianity is not a "cookie-cutter" or top-heavy authoritative institution. We acknowledge the three basic branches of the Church—the Eastern Orthodox, the Roman Catholic, and the Protestant—besides some interesting groups that identify with none of the above. Despite differences, we all hold to the Triune God, the author of our Holy Bible, who provided the only means of salvation in our redeemer, the Lord Jesus Christ.

To this Holy Trinity we owe our devotion and praise.

Section I:
The Basic Lessons

Part I:
The God Who Reveals Himself

Lesson One

The God of the Bible

Note: The Bible is not arranged like a systematic theology book. Information about the Creator, the Maker of heaven and earth, is scattered from Genesis to Revelation. God actually reveals and defines Himself in His words and His deeds. Our methodology is to gather the pieces of God's self revelation under broad themes. These will be God's sovereignty, holiness, and tri-unity.

A.   The Creator God is Sovereign

  1. Sovereign means that the God revealed in Scripture is almighty. He has done and will do what pleases Himself.
  2. God is omnipotent, or all-powerful. God is omniscient, or all-knowing. God is omnipresent, or all-present.
  3. There is nothing above or beyond God. He has no equal.
  4. God is infinite, immaterial, invisible, eternal, self-existent, transcendent, immanent, unchangeable, Spirit, love, Person, and far more than can be expressed by words. (There will be some overlap in the meanings of some of

these attributes of God.)

5. Examine: Genesis 1:1, 1:27; Exodus 3:14; John 1:14, 4:24; Isaiah 55:9; 1 John 4:8; 1 Timothy 6:16.

B. **The Creator God is Holy**

1. Holy means set apart.
2. Holy means without sin; sin is that which is not in accord with the nature of God; it is the breaking of the Law of God as revealed in Scripture. The words "transgression" and "inequity" are close synonyms of sin but differ slightly.
3. Holy means perfection.
4. Because God is holy, He is also righteous and just. God acts toward His creation righteously and justly. He is the Judge of all humankind. God will judge sin. Jesus, the Son of God, is our righteousness.
5. Examine Exodus 3:1–6; Habakkuk 1:13; Matthew 5:48; Hebrews 7:26; 1 Peter 1:13–16, 2:24; Romans 3:10, 6:23; 1 Corinthians 15:3; and 2 Corinthians 5:21.

C. **The Creator God is Triune**

1. God is a unity—a unity of three—a Trinity.
2. The Law affirms that God is one, which is the foundation of monotheism, and that oneness is a unity of three.
3. In Genesis 2:24 and Deuteronomy 6:4, the word "one" is echad.
    a. "Therefore a man shall leave his father and his mother and hold fast to his wife, and they shall become one flesh" (Genesis 2:24)
    b. "Hear, O Israel: The LORD our God, the LORD is one" (Deuteronomy 6:4).
4. Combining the information about God in the two pas-

sages, it is evident that Adam and Eve together were an echad and God is an echad. God is an echad—a trinity or three-in-one. That God reveals Himself[1] as Father, Son, and Holy Spirit is not then an expression of three deities. Here is a clear look at a paradox, of which there are many in the Scripture. The trinity is one yet three, three yet one.

5. Examine Genesis 1:2, 1:26, 11:7; Isaiah 7:14, 9:6, 63:10; Matthew 28:19; Luke 3:21–22; John 10:30, 14:8–9; 1 Corinthians 2:11; 2 Corinthians 13:14; Ephesians 2:18; and 1 Peter 1:2.

---

1   God is both male and female at once, which is clear from Genesis 1:27: "So God created man in his own image, in the image of God he created him; male and female he created them." Translators and editors have traditionally and customarily used the male personal pronoun for God rather than employ a clumsier and complicated means of referring to the God of Scripture. Please note also that in the current work, the author capitalizes pronouns referring to God, while the editors of the English Standard Version of the Bible quoted in the Christian Basics do not do so.

Lesson Two

Revelation

Revelation is God's acting to make Himself known. The Word of God is the apex of God's revelation, both Jesus Christ—the living Word—and the Bible—the written Word of God. A thing is either hidden or revealed. God has chosen to reveal Himself rather than be hidden.

Knowledge of God exists only as far as God has revealed Himself. The writer of Hebrews speaks to this: "Long ago, at many times and in many ways, God spoke to our fathers by the prophets, but in these last days he has spoken to us by his Son" (Hebrews 1:2a).

God is more awesome and almighty than is humanly possible to grasp. We are very limited in our understanding. For instance, God knows the end from the beginning, which makes prophecy possible. The prophecies about the Messiah in the Old Testament are sprinkled throughout it and have been shown to be exactly accurate, because the actual events unfolded as God planned. The prophecy did not determine the event; God, knowing all things at once, described ahead of time through the prophets what He would do. Anything less than this is a 'god' who does not know the end from the beginning, essentially an idol and no God.

A.   General and Special Revelation

1. General revelation means that knowledge of God is potentially common or available to all humans. Paul wrote,

    For what can be known about God is plain to them, because God has shown it to them. For his invisible attributes, namely, his eternal power and divine nature, have been clearly perceived ever since the creation of the world, in the things that have been made. So they are without excuse. (Romans 1:19-20)

2. God is revealed in His creation—the things He has made. In addition, God is known to us via our mind, heart, or conscience. Though this is a complex issue, Paul's instruction to Titus summarizes the essential points:

    To the pure, all things are pure, but to the defiled and unbelieving, nothing is pure; but both their minds and their consciences are defiled. (Titus 1:15)

3. An example of God's truth and reality is somehow encoded in us—like a built-in spiritual DNA. The conscience, which means "with knowledge," may be how the Creator worked it out. The emotion of guilt is most often related to sinful behavior. Even when the culture condones certain behavior, the conscience will not.

4. Some knowledge of God as Creator is common to all humans, but the exact nature of God is neither evident nor uniform among the peoples and tribes of the earth. This is one reason why there are so many different and conflicting religious worldviews.

5. Special revelation means that there is a knowledge of God not common or available to all humans that must be particularly revealed by God Himself.

a. As we saw in Hebrews 1:2a, Jesus Himself is that special revelation. This is the subject of John's prologue in John 1:1–18. The key verses are,

In the beginning was the Word, and the Word was with God, and the Word was God (verse 1). And the Word became flesh and dwelt among us, and we have seen his glory, glory as of the only Son from the Father, full of grace and truth (verse 14). No one has ever seen God; the only God, who is at the Father's side, he has made him known (verse 18).

b. The Bible is the record of special revelation. This may not be evident in the early stages of a Christian's experience, but as the years pass the inward proving of the Bible as God's inspired Word grows and blossoms.

B. Objective versus Subjective Revelation

1. Objective revelation means that God has revealed Himself, whether or not that revelation is received or accepted. Humans do not create truth, however sincerely they hold concepts and ideas.

2. Subjective revelation is the work of God wherein He purposefully reveals His Son Jesus Christ to a person by the agency of the Holy Spirit. This revelation becomes personal.

3. Subjective revelation highlights the working of the Triune God. God the Father is the author of all that is revealed; He reveals His Son by the inner working of the Holy Spirit in the life, mind, and conscience of those who are regenerated or born anew. This is a life-long process and comes by means of the reading of and meditating on Scripture, prayer, hearing instruction by the Church's preachers and teachers, and by the day-by-day experience of being an obedient disciple and follower of Jesus.

Lesson Three

Scripture

Scripture for Christians is comprised of the Old and New Testaments, from Genesis to Revelation.[1]
Together the Old and New Testaments make up what is called the Bible, from the Greek word meaning book. Scripture is a word that means writing, but not just any writing; this is special, sacred, or inspired writing whose author is the Maker of heaven and earth.

Christians believe the Old and New testaments—contracts, agreements, or covenants—are inspired or "God breathed."

---

1 Roman Catholics and others include in their canon of Scripture books known as the Apocrypha. The Greek translation of the Old Testament commonly known as the LXX (Septuagint) included these books when the Jewish scholars in Alexandria, Egypt, early in the second century before Christ, translated the Hebrew Bible into Greek. Jerome, who then translated the Hebrew and Greek testaments into Latin, used the LXX. Thus the Apocryphal books were included, and thus this translation became the official edition of the Bible for Roman Catholics. Centuries later Protestants excluded these books from their editions of the Bible, since the orthodox Palestinian Jews also did not accept them into their canon.

This is largely a matter of faith but also of experience. Paul wrote to Timothy that "All Scripture is breathed out by God and profitable for teaching, for reproof, correction, and for training in righteousness, that the man of God may be competent, equipped for every good work" (2 Timothy 3:10–17).

Notice the word "breathed," translated from a Greek word that is literally rendered "God-Spirited." Paul was referring to the Hebrew Bible, or the Tanakh, or the Old Testament, from Genesis to Malachi, but by extension the New Testament, since the Old Testament points toward the coming of the Messiah, Jesus Christ. "God breathed" has been applied by the Church from its very beginning to the New Testament as well, from Matthew to Revelation.

The Bible is God's objective revelation. It is God's true Word, whether believed upon or not. Jesus said, "Heaven and earth will pass away, but my words will not pass away" (Luke 21:33).

The Bible is therefore the Christian's sole authority for faith and practice, that is, for what we believe and do.

The Bible remains the Church's sole authority, yet it has been variously interpreted. Doctrines and practice impact and influence interpretation, certainly, but tradition and practice must not stand as sole authority for what is believed and practiced. Generally, only Protestants hold to this single source of authority, since the Eastern Orthodox, Roman Catholic, and Anglican (Episcopal in America) churches include as authoritative both tradition (the decisions of councils) and pronouncements by the heads of the Church.

Determining what is authoritative must be solidly rooted in the whole of Scripture. A good rule of thumb to determine the authority and truth of any doctrine is that it must be plainly seen in the Old Testament, and preferably all three segments of it—the Torah, the Prophets, and the Writings; then in the Gospels—Matthew, Mark, Luke, and John; and finally or additionally in the testimony of the early Church—in the letters of the New Testament from the Book of Acts to Revelation.

Note: Doctrines are points of a theology. Theology literally means God (theo) plus the word (logos). Doctrines, in combination, form a theology. You can observe that the theology of Scripture contains a number of doctrines.

There is no objective method to prove that the Bible is inspired by God, although several passages declare as much. A document cannot be used to infallibly prove its own authority, which constitutes a "cyclical argument." That the Bible is the inspired Word of God is a statement of faith. **Far above any external verification of the Bible is the inner witness of the Holy Spirit.** Though easy to say, there is no scientific test to back it up, but Christians come to a position on Scripture with more confidence than could be arrived at by any scientific or historical demonstration.

Lesson Four

The Old Testament

The Old Testament may also be referred to as the Torah, the Tanakh, the Hebrew Bible, or the Hebrew Scripture. The language of the Old Testament is Hebrew except for several passages which are Aramaic. Aramaic uses the same Semitic alphabet but is distinct from Hebrew.

There are thirty-nine books in the Christian traditional layout of the Old Testament, but the count is different in an edition conforming to Judaism. For instance, Christian Bible editions count 1 Samuel and 2 Samuel as two, but in a Jewish edition they are combined as Samuel. The same is true of Kings and Chronicles. In the Hebrew Bible, Chronicles is the final book, while in Christian editions the last book is Malachi.

This lesson is intended to acquaint the reader with only the general make-up of the Old Testament. Learning it in depth requires a lifetime at minimum, but understanding its basics is utterly necessary in order to have a proper understanding of the New Testament.

A. **The Major Sections**
1. The **Torah**, or **Pentateuch**, is comprised of the "Five Books of Moses": Genesis, Exodus, Leviticus, Numbers, and Deuteronomy. These are the first five books of the Old Testament.
   a. The dates for the writing of the Pentateuch are uncertain but are between the fifteenth and the thirteenth centuries BC, i.e., from about 1450 BC to about 1250 BC. Some scholars date these books much later, some even earlier, but the precise date of authorship is illusive and debatable.
   b. The author is traditionally said to be Moses, but obviously the last section of Deuteronomy could not have been written by Moses, since it describes his death. Some scholars suggest that other scribes, working over many centuries, were involved in the final preparation of the books. Both liberal and conservative scholars agree on this, but no view prevents the God-breathing that transforms the books into sacred Scripture.
2. The **Historical Books** are Joshua, Judges, Ruth, 1 Samuel, 2 Samuel, 1 Kings, 2 Kings, 1 Chronicles, 2 Chronicles, Ezra, Nehemiah, and Esther.
   a. The dates for these books generally run from the fourteenth to the fourth centuries BC; however, each book's date must be considered separately.
   b. The authors are rarely known, and many guesses have been made, but in the books themselves no author is stated.
3. The **Poetic and Wisdom Books** are Job, Psalms, Proverbs, Ecclesiastes, and Song of Solomon.
   a. The dates for these books generally fit into the tenth

Christian Basics

to eighth centuries B.C, that is, from 900 BC to 700 BC.

   b. The books are mostly authored by David, Solomon, and others unnamed, but all come out of the community of Israel.

4. The Prophetic Books are Isaiah, Jeremiah, Lamentations, Ezekiel, Daniel, Hosea, Joel, Amos, Obadiah, Jonah, Micah, Nahum, Habakkuk, Zephaniah, Haggai, Zechariah, and Malachi.

   a. The dates of authorship vary from the eighth to the fourth century.

   b. The authors may actually be the very persons whose names appear in the books themselves, or the author may be a secretary of the named prophet, as in the case of Jeremiah (though Jeremiah most likely dictated the content).

B.   The Major Themes

Running throughout the Old Testament are several themes, all centered on who God is, what He has done, and what He has planned and promised for His people in the future:

1. God is creator—by what means is not stated, except that God is directly in control and sovereign.

2. God is personal—He communicates with His creation that He made in His own image. He set boundaries and acted in judgment when these were violated.

3. God is a lawgiver who establishes covenants or agreements with those whom He calls to Himself.

4. God is holy—utterly separated from sin, demanding holiness from those He created.

5. God is steadfast in His love for His people and provides a means for their redemption. His commandments and a

sacrificial system are the center of His redemptive plan.
6. God sends prophets to warn and guide His people.
7. Two Messiahs are evident in the Old Testament: Messiah Son of Joseph is the suffering servant of Israel, and Messiah Son of David is the mighty warrior king.

Lesson Five

The New Testament

The New Testament is comprised of twenty-seven books. Most of these are letters, or epistles (*epistole* is the Greek word for letter). The epistles were more than letters and ushered in a new type of biblical literature, since they laid out key doctrines of the Christian faith. Four of the books are Gospels, or messages of Good News. Gospel is a Middle English word that means "good message." Following the Gospels comes a book of history known as Acts. And the last book of the Bible, Revelation, is a different genre all together, being an apocalyptic book, a book of revealing that which had been hidden.

The New Testament is written in Greek, some of it very polished Greek. Historically, there is classical Greek, common or Koine Greek, and modern Greek. Koine is the kind of Greek we find in the New Testament.

This lesson is intended to acquaint one with the general make-up of the New Testament. For many, if not most Christians, it becomes a rich and constant source of inspiration, guidance, and encouragement.

A.   **The Major Sections**

1. The **Gospels** are Matthew, Mark, Luke, and John. The first three—Matthew, Mark, and Luke—are referred to as the synoptic Gospels, because they have a similar account of the life and ministry of Jesus. John's Gospel is more of a theological treatment of the life and teachings of Jesus. Matthew and John were called apostles (two of the Twelve Disciples originally called by Jesus); Mark was Peter's companion, and thus his Gospel is sometimes referred to as Peter's Gospel; and Luke was Paul's companion. Thus the Gospels were written either by an apostle or a disciple of an apostle.

    a. The dates for the writing of the Gospels vary. It is thought Mark was written first, perhaps as early as A.D. 50, but likely later. Matthew's and Luke's Gospels may be dated in the 60s. At minimum, these three synoptic Gospels, according to most biblical scholars, were written before the destruction of Jerusalem and the Temple in A.D. 70. Dates for John's Gospel vary from A.D. 88 to A.D. 95.

    b. There are no original manuscripts of any Gospel extant today, and thus there are no signature originals. No apostle or disciple of an apostle signed a Gospel nor directly indicated authorship. Tradition, coupled with biblical analysis, substantially indicates who the authors are. There are some who dispute both authorship and/or dating, but generally there is a consistent agreement about both.

2. Following the Gospels is the book of **Acts**. Luke, who wrote the third Gospel, also wrote Acts, and tradition and biblical sleuthing or analysis confirms this.

    a. The date of the writing of Acts is usually stated to be from A.D. 62 to 65. Since there is no mention in either Luke or Acts of the destruction of Jerusalem or even mention of the Jewish rebellion against Rome that began in A.D. 66, it is easily assumed that both documents were written before A.D. 66.

3. The **letters of Paul** are Romans, 1 Corinthians, 2 Corinthians, Galatians, Ephesians, Philippians, Colossians, 1 Thessalonians, 2 Thessalonians, 1 Timothy, 2 Timothy, Titus, and Philemon.

   a. The dates for these books vary greatly, from about A.D. 49 for Galatians, likely the first letter Paul wrote, to the two letters to Timothy that may date to A.D. 65 or a little later. There is a continuing debate as to the dates of Paul's letters. The content of the conversation involving them is complex.

   b. The authorship of the thirteen letters above is generally and traditionally ascribed to Paul. The letters to Timothy are questioned more than the others.

4. The Letter to the **Hebrews**.

   a. The date for Hebrews is unknown, but it was likely written before the destruction of the Temple at Jerusalem in A.D. 70. It is thought such an event would have been at least mentioned in Hebrews.

   b. The author of Hebrews is unknown. Prior to the last few decades, it was traditionally credited to Paul, but stylistic issues preclude Paul's authorship. Scholars have proposed the author variously to be Barnabas, Apollos, Silas, and Aquila and Priscilla, among others. Hebrews is the best example of polished Greek writing in the New Testament.

5. **James**

   a. The author is likely James, half-brother of Jesus who is mentioned in the Gospels and Acts. He became the first pastor of the Jerusalem Church and directed the Council of Jerusalem as recorded in Acts 15.

b. The date of James could be as early as A.D. 45, making it possibly the earliest Christian document. James died in A.D. 62.

6. 1 and 2 Peter

a. The authorship of 1 Peter is debated but is fairly well agreed upon. In the opening sentence, 1 Peter 1:1, the author identifies himself as Peter and states he was an eye witness to the sufferings of Jesus. The same is true for 2 Peter, which has even a stronger case for Peter's authorship than 1 Peter. Traditionally both letters are ascribed to Peter, yet the debate over both letters will likely continue.

b. The date of 1 Peter may be A.D. 62 or 63. Most scholars agree that Peter died during the rule of Nero, A.D. 54–68, and probably, according to tradition, died by crucifixion, which he himself requested to be done upside down, anywhere from A.D. 64 to 67. It is speculated that Peter wrote 2 Peter shortly before his martyrdom.

7. Jude

a. The author is the brother of James and half-brother of Jesus. There is little disagreement over the authorship.

b. There is a close similarity between Jude and 2 Peter, and the date of Jude is reckoned to be close to the date of 2 Peter, thus about A.D. 65.

8. 1, 2, and 3 John and the Book of **Revelation**

a. The author of all four books, the first three being letters, is the apostle John. 3 John is often debated as to authorship, but tradition holds to John. The author of both 2 and 3 John is said to be "the elder," and this elder is likely John. In the prologue to Revelation, chapter 1 and verse 1, the writer says he is John. There is strong evidence that all three letters and Revelation were written by John in the 90s.

B. **The Major Themes of the New Testament**

1. The Word, who is God, became flesh and actually lived among people.

2. The Word, or Logos, is Jesus of Nazareth, born of the Virgin Mary in Bethlehem. This event marks the beginning of the designation, A.D. or Anno Domini ("year of the Lord") after the Lord's birth.[1]

3. Jesus is a direct descendant from Abraham, Isaac, and Jacob, then through the tribe of Judah, son of Jacob, and also through the clan of King David, thus fulfilling the prophecies spoken of for the Messiah.

4. Jesus is the Christ, with "Christ" being the Greek form for the Hebrew *Meshiach*, meaning Messiah or anointed one. He called disciples, taught them over the course of three to five years, healed the sick, cast out demons, raised the dead, commanded nature, multiplied organic matter, and was then betrayed, arrested, condemned, and crucified—all in accordance with Old Testament prophecy.

5. Jesus was raised from the dead on a Sunday, appeared to His disciples over the course of forty days, and then ascended to heaven from whence He had come.

6. Jesus established His Church, for which He promised to return at the close of the age.

---

1   The dating system has a flaw in that Jesus was born before the death of Herod the Great, who died in 4 BC. Probably Jesus was born around 6 BC in our present dating system.

Lesson Six

How We Got the Bible

Human beings wrote the Bible—real people and not angels or any other spiritual being.

A.   General Understandings

1. God chose and inspired imperfect people to write His Word. Therefore, we say that the Bible is inspired by God, or God-breathed, and this belief is an article of faith rather than an empirically proven fact.

2. We distinguish between the living Word, who is Jesus, and the written Word, which is the Bible.

3. A vital understanding of the Bible is that it is an "Eastern" and not a "Western" document. This means the Bible differs from what the Western mindset expects, which is that all things must match perfectly without variation at all. Examples of this are in the Synoptic Gospels—Matthew, Mark, and Luke. The same stories appear in each of them, but they differ in detail, sometimes significantly.

This did not bother the authors or the early Christians for many centuries. When Christianity was absorbed into the Western mindset some scribes attempted to harmonize the Gospels, but these variants are not accepted in the modern editions of Scripture. The study of the formation of the New Testament is complex but extremely interesting. It is a valuable undertaking for all Christians to take a close look at the origins of their New Testament.

4. The Bible is a spiritual book, and without the aid of the Holy Spirit no one can adequately understand it. Paul put it this way: "The natural man does not accept the things of the Spirit of God, for they are folly to him, and he is not able to understand them because they are spiritually discerned" (1 Corinthians 2:14).

5. A Christian's grasp and understanding of the Bible grows as he or she encounters it, studies it, and learns to love it.

B. The Development of the Old Testament

1. The Books of Genesis, Exodus, Leviticus, Numbers, and Deuteronomy were the first to be called inspired, since they owed their origin to Moses, the prophet empowered by God to bring the children of Israel out of slavery in Egypt and to whom God gave His Law. This did not happen immediately, but as is true of all the books of the Bible, their acceptance developed over the centuries.

2. The historical books—Joshua, Judges, Ruth, 1 and 2 Samuel, 1 and 2 Kings, 1 and 2 Chronicles, Ezra, Nehemiah, and Esther—were valued by Israel, as they recorded the essential histories of God's people. In time, these books also were viewed as sacred Scripture.

3. The books of the prophets, from Isaiah to Malachi, beginning in the ninth century BC, began to be viewed as Scripture, since the words the prophets spoke and which were

then subsequently written down, were words from God.

4. The Writings of Job, Psalms, Proverbs, Ecclesiastes, and the Song of Solomon were written by the great kings of Israel (except Job) and therefore had a special place for Israel.

5. The order of books accepted as sacred and inspired by God were first, the books of Moses, then the historical books, the prophetic books, and finally, not until the Christian Era had begun, the writings.

C. **The Development of the New Testament**

1. The New Testament books were viewed as Scripture from around the middle of the second century AD, or AD 150. However, the formation of the basic books came prior to that time. It is difficult to say precisely, because there were no church councils during those early days to make any definitive statements.

2. The books written by apostles or disciples of apostles, like Matthew, Mark, Luke, and John, were much valued by the early Church and so were collected and used in churches all over the Mediterranean region. As the generation of Christians matured who were alive during the ministry of Jesus, it became necessary for the life and times of Jesus to be recorded both for teaching and missionary work.

3. Luke's Gospel, and Acts especially, made Paul a well-known figure, and local churches began to collect his letters and use them for discipleship and evangelistic purposes. James and Jude found acceptance in the early Church due to their relationship to their half-brother Jesus, and also in James' case, his leadership in the early days of the Church.

D. **Canonization**

1. The story of the development of the "canon" of the New Testament is a fascinating one. Essentially, the books that had apostolic connections were readily received, whereas a myriad of false writings that began turning up in Gnostic circles were rejected.
2. Very similar to the canonization process of the Old Testament, the content of the New Testament grew slowly, but by the middle of the second century, the makeup of the New Testament was generally accepted and understood.
3. With both testaments, the process is often viewed as a winnowing one whereby the Holy Spirit impressed upon the faithful communities what were and what were not authoritative and reliable words from God.

Lesson Seven

The Great Paradoxes of the Bible

paradox: the Greek parts of this word are *para*, as in parallel, like railroad tracks that lie side by side but never meet; and *dox*, as in truth. A paradox refers to two truths that are parallel to each other but never meet, although we wish they would. And because the paradoxes cannot be resolved, they create unease in us, a tension that forces us to hold both to be true at once.

It is not possible to thoroughly outline and explain the many paradoxes we discover in Scripture, nor is it possible to examine all the passages of Scripture that bear on the paradoxes presented in this lesson. We have already observed one of the most significant paradoxes of the Bible, that of the two Messiahs—Messiah Son of Joseph and Messiah Son of David. The suffering servant of Israel and the mighty warrior king are much different from each other, but both are true at once.

A. **The two-fold nature of Jesus**

    1. Jesus is both God and man at once. To deny one or the other would drastically alter the central core of the Gos-

pel message.

2. As God, Jesus is the perfect and sinless Lamb of God, providing the atonement for sin in His death. As man, Jesus does actually die, receiving upon Himself our sin, guilt, and judgment.

3. Relevant passages: Genesis 3:15; Psalm 22; Isaiah 7:14, 9:6, 53:1–12; Philippians 2:5–11; Colossians 1:15–20.

B.   The two-fold nature of the Bible

1. The Bible is written by people who were fallible.

2. The Bible is written or inspired by God, who is not fallible.

3. In the Bible we observe this duality; we see the hand of God and the hand of humans.

4. Relevant passages: 2 Timothy 3:16–17; 2 Peter 1:19–21.

C.   The paradox of prayer

1. God knows our needs before we ask Him.

2. We are to pray nevertheless.

3. Relevant passages: Matthew 6:8, 7:7; Romans 8:26; Philippians 4:6; Hebrews 4:16.

D.   The paradox of the resurrection[1]

1. We will be raised from the dead at the second coming of Christ.

2. At the moment of our death we are in the presence of God.

3. Relevant passages: Job 19:25–27; Psalm 49:15; Isaiah 25:8, 26:19; Daniel 12:2; Hosea 13:14; Matthew 17:1–

---

1   Some, like C.S. Lewis, resolve this by suggesting that when a person dies he or she leaves the boundaries of chronological time and enters God's time, kairos, making both sides of the paradox actual at once.

Section I: Part I: Lesson 7: Great Paradoxes of the Bible

13; Luke 23:43; 2 Corinthians 5:1–8; Philippians 1:23; 1 Thessalonians 4:13-18.

E. **God's election and the necessity of repenting and believing (also known as the paradox of grace verses works).**[2]

1. God elects for salvation from eternity, before the foundation of the earth.
2. People must repent and believe.
3. Relevant passages: John 3:16, 6:40, 44; Acts 16:31; Romans 8:30, 10:9–11, 10:17; Ephesians 2:8–9.

F. **The God of love and the God of judgment**

1. The God of the Bible, the creator of heaven and earth, is a God of love.
2. The God of the Bible is a God of wrath and judgment, both inside of history and outside of history.
3. Relevant passages: Matthew 25:31–46; John 3:16–21, 5:25–29; Romans 5:8–9; 1 John 4:10; Revelation 20:11–15.

G. **Christians are perfectly and completely forgiven yet are sinners at the same time.**

1. In Christ our sin has been removed.
2. Yet sin dwells within us.
3. Relevant passages: Romans 5:1, 6:11–14, 7:7–25, 8:1, 33–34, 2 Corinthians 5:17; Hebrews 12:1–2; 1 John 1:8–2:2.

H. **Christians are at once free and slaves.**

1. We are free from death and sin in Christ.

---

2 This paradox is often resolved by arguing that God provides the ability to repent and believe, and thus salvation is in no way dependent on human thought or action.

2. We are slaves of Christ

3. Relevant passages: Romans 6:1–23; Galatians 2:20, 5:1.

I. The paradox of the Lord's Supper

1. The bread and the cup are the actual body and blood of Christ: the sacramental concept.

2. The bread and the cup represent Christ's body and blood: the ordinance concept.

3. Relevant passages: Matthew 26:26–29; John 1:12, 6:41–59; 1 Corinthians 11:23–26.

J. The paradox of striving and resting

1. In Christ we "rest" from our labor.

2. In Christ we are striving.

3. Relevant passages: Matthew 11:28; Ephesians 1:19, 2:6, 2:10, 6:10–18; 1 Corinthians 15:10; Colossians 1:24–29.

Section I, Continued:

The Basic Lessons

Part 2:

The Great Themes of the Bible

Lesson Eight

Election

The doctrine of election generally states that God Himself is responsible for an individual's salvation.

A. Theological terms from Scripture

1. Foreknowledge, predestination, election, calling, justifying, glorifying—these are the work of God and are the terms that describe the parts or process of our salvation.

For those whom he foreknew he also predestined to be conformed to the image of his Son, in order that he might be the firstborn among many brothers. And those whom he predestined he also called, and those whom he called he also justified, and those whom he justified he also glorified. (Romans 8:29–30)

2. Although the word "elect" or "election" is not found specifically in this passage describing the sovereign work of God, it is the perfect and unifying term that sums it all up.

3. From the Hebrew Old Testament, *baw-khir* is the trans-

literated form for the word that is translated as choose, chosen one, or elect. Isaiah used the term in 42:1, 45:4, 65:9, and 65:22 to describe Israel. Israel was selected by God to be His own people; the people themselves did not choose God.

4. From the Greek New Testament, *eklektos* and *ekloge* are the transliterated forms for the words that are translated as choose, elect, select, or choice. Jesus used eklektos in Matthew 24:22, 24:24, and 24:31; they are also found uttered by Jesus in Mark 13:20, 13:22, and 13:27; then also in Luke 18:7, all in reference to those whom God had chosen.

5. Paul used the terms in Romans 8:33, Colossians 3:12, 1 Thessalonians 1:4, 1 Timothy 5:21, 2 Timothy 2:10, and Titus 1:1. Peter used the terms in 1 Peter 1:2 and 1:6, 1 Peter 5:13, and 2 Peter 1:10. John used one of the terms in 2 John 1 and 13.

6. Election is how it is that God calls us to Himself—His foreknowing, predestinating, calling, justifying, and glorifying—all under the grand and large umbrella of election.

B. **Biblical support for the Reformed position**

1. The **Old Testament** is full of examples of election. These may be referred to as prophetic historical dramas.

    a. God acted sovereignly in choosing Abel over Cain, and Cain was the firstborn who would have been the chief inheritor of Adam's estate. It should be noted that by ancient tradition within early human societies, the firstborn generally inherited the father's estate.

    b. Noah and his family were chosen to be preserved over everyone else.

c. Abram (later renamed Abraham by God) was an 'Abru or Hebrew, a member of a small Semitic clan and was chosen rather than others. Late in the third millennium before Christ, there were many great nations and warriors present, all of which were more powerful and important than Abram.

d. Isaac, who was Abraham and Sarah's son, was the child of promise, and though he was the second-born, he was nevertheless chosen to be in the line of the Messiah over Ishmael, the son of Abraham and Hagar.

e. Isaac had two sons, Esau and Jacob, and once again Jacob was chosen, although Esau was the firstborn.

f. The Chosen People of God—Israel—was chosen over all the tribes on the earth as the people through whom the Messiah would come. This is election from start to finish.

2. The **New Testament** continues the theme of election from the Old Testament. The following passages show this:

"For many are called, but few are chosen" (Matthew 22:14).

"You did not choose me, but I chose you and appointed you that you should go and bear fruit and that your fruit should abide, so that whatever you ask the Father in my name, he may give it to you" (John 15:16).

"All that the Father gives me will come to me, and whoever comes to me I will never cast out" (John 6:37).

"No one can come to me unless the Father who sent me draws him" (John 6:44).

"And when the Gentiles heard this, they began rejoicing and glorifying the word of the Lord, and as many as were appointed to eternal life believed" (Acts 13:48).

"For those whom he foreknew he also predestined to be conformed to the image of his Son, in order that he might be the firstborn among many brothers. And those whom he predestined he also called, and those whom he called he also justified, and those whom he justified he also glorified" (Romans 8:29–30).

"Even as he chose us in him before the foundation of the world, that we should be holy and blameless before him" (Ephesians 1:4).

"But we ought always to give thanks to God for you, brothers beloved by the Lord, because God chose you as the first fruits to be saved, through sanctification by the Spirit and belief in the truth" (2 Thessalonians 2:13).

"Who saved us and called us to a holy calling, not because of our works but because of his own purpose and grace, which he gave us in Christ Jesus before the ages began" (2 Timothy 1:9).

And there are many more.

C.   Unconditional Election

1. Election is not election if there are any conditions. Salvation would be a reward or wage that is earned, if there were any conditions required.

2. There is no grace if salvation is dependent upon a human being. Grace is God's doing what we cannot do.

3. Election is also embedded in the metaphor of the new birth as described in John chapter three. "You must be born again," or according to the literal Greek, "you must be born from above" (see John 3:1–15). It is abundantly

clear that we are not involved with our own birth except for being there. We had nothing to do with the conception, gestation, or birthing. Likewise, with the new birth we are not involved. Jesus went on to make it clear that the new birth, which one must receive in order to see the kingdom of God, was solely a work of God through His Spirit.

4. Jesus was speaking of unconditional election without using the term. John referenced the concept again in his first epistle: "Everyone who believes that Jesus is the Christ has been born of God, and everyone who loves the Father loves whoever has been born of him" (1 John 5:1).

5. It is clear which is the proper order: first the birth from God then the believing. This is an essential point, as it reveals the unconditional nature of salvation. We cannot believe, will not believe, do not believe, without the new birth.

Lesson Nine

Presence

The Bible opens as God is creating the universe. Occupying center stage are human beings who are created in His image. *Image*—this word is considered by most commentators to mean that God created men and women with the capacity to communicate or commune with Him. Another way to express this is that we are created as soul, as spiritual,[1] and thus can have a relationship with our Creator.

A. In His Presence

In Genesis 1:28 we read, "And God blessed them. And God said to them, 'Be fruitful and multiply and fill the earth and subdue it.'" Notice the words, "God said to them." The first humans, Adam and Eve,[2] were in the presence of their Creator, convers-

---

1 Only humans are soul and spiritual; no other thing is so created.
2 As to the literal interpretation of Adam and Eve, some will take it thus, and others will interpret it symbolically. Some of the finest biblically oriented scholars vary widely. Often Christians will change their minds on this issue as they go along. A particular viewpoint does not make one a liberal or a conservative.

ing with Him. No conversation took place with any other part of what God created, including the animals.

Then in Genesis 2:15–17:

> The LORD God took the man and put him in the Garden of Eden to work it and keep it. And the LORD God commanded the man, saying, "You may surely eat of every tree of the garden, but the tree of the knowledge of good and evil you shall not eat, for in the day that you eat of it you shall surely die."[3]

Once again there is a conversation between God and man,[4] in this case Adam. A few verses further on in chapter two, God asks Adam to name the animals (verse 19). Again there is conversation, making it clear that God is right there present with the man.

Moving to chapter three of Genesis to what followed after the Fall, the breaking of God's single command not to eat of the tree of the knowledge of good and evil, is a passage that goes to the core of the issue:

> And they heard the sound of the LORD God walking in the garden in the cool of the day, and the man and his wife hid themselves from the presence of the LORD God among the trees of the garden. But the LORD God called to the man and said to him, "Where are you?" And he said, "I heard the sound of you in the garden, and I was afraid, because I was naked, and I hid myself." He said, "Who told you that you were naked? Have you eaten of the tree of which I commanded you not to eat?" The man said, "The woman whom you gave to be with me, she gave me fruit of the tree, and I ate." Then the LORD God said to the woman, "What is this that you have

---

3   Adam and Eve did not die a physical death but suffered worse—they experienced separation from God, a spiritual death.

4   The use of the term "man" is inclusive of men and women.

done?" The woman said, "The serpent deceived me, and I ate." (Genesis 3:8-13)

It is clear that Adam and Eve were in the presence of God. Due to their disobedience, however, that changed.

B.   East of Eden—No longer in the Presence of God

The single most catastrophic event the world has ever known had taken place:

> The LORD God sent him out from the Garden of Eden to work the ground from which he was taken. He drove out the man, and at the east of the Garden of Eden he placed the cherubim and a flaming sword that turned every way to guard the way to the tree of life. (Genesis 3:23-24)

God and man were now separated, since God is holy, and no sin can be in His presence. The long history of humankind began, all of which has been characterized by our not being in His presence.

The dominant storyline of Scripture is that God acts to bring us back into His presence. The story's focal point is the Messiah, the One whose work it is to abolish sin and its power of separation. The center of the story is the Cross and the shed blood of the Lamb, which alone has the power to cover our sin.

C.   In His Presence (Again)

The Bible concludes with humans, those redeemed by the blood of the Lamb,[5] back in the presence of God, which is the ultimate intention of the Creator.

Two passages from the Book of Revelation declare the dramatic conclusion to the cosmic story:

> Then I saw a new heaven and a new earth, for the first

---

[5]   It was the blood of the animal sacrifices on the altar that atoned for or covered sin. "The blood of the Lamb" is the blood shed by Jesus, the sacrificial or Passover Lamb of God that covers human sin.

heaven and the first earth had passed away, and the sea was no more. And I saw the holy city, new Jerusalem, coming down out of heaven from God, prepared as a bride adorned for her husband. And I heard a loud voice from the throne saying, "Behold, the dwelling place of God is with man. He will be with them, and they will be his people, and God himself will be with them as their God. He will wipe away every tear from their eyes, and death shall be no more, neither shall there be mourning nor crying nor pain anymore, for the former things have passed away." (Revelation 21:1–4)

No longer will there be anything accursed, but the throne of God and of the Lamb will be in it, and his servants will worship him. They will see his face, and his name will be on their foreheads. And night will be no more. They will need no light of lamp or sun, for the LORD God will be their light, and they will reign forever and ever. (Revelation 22:3–5)

Lesson Ten

Rest

The concept of the presence of God and the "rest" He gives the believer are closely linked together.

A.   The Day of Rest: Sabbath

As with "presence," it is also in Genesis that the great theme of "rest" is found. The day of rest is the seventh day. For the first six, God did the "work" of creating, then on the seventh He ceased working and "rested."[1]

> Thus the heavens and the earth were finished, and all the host of them. And on the seventh day God finished his work that he had done, and he rested on the seventh day from all his work that he had done. So God blessed the seventh day and made it holy, because on it God

---

1   "Rest" is what humans do; to speak of God as resting is to use the literary device called anthropomorphism, that is, ascribing to God human characteristics. In Scripture it does not mean that God literally rested but that He ceased doing something, and in regard to Genesis, it is to cease from creating.

rested from all his work that he had done in creation. (Genesis 2:1–3)

The fourth commandment of the Law has to do with the seventh day, known as the Sabbath day. The first two verses of the fourth commandment are, "Remember the Sabbath day, to keep it holy. Six days you shall labor, and do all your work, but the seventh day is a Sabbath to the LORD your God" (Exodus 20:8–9).

The word "sabbath" (from the Hebrew *shabbat*) means rest. For the Jewish people the seventh day begins on Friday at sunset and ends on Saturday at sunset. Over the centuries many other laws were developed by Jewish scholars and rabbis to make sure the Sabbath Day would be properly observed.[2]

B. Historical Dramatic Prophecy

Sabbath rest is more than an observance and commandment; it is a central theme of the Bible. To rest is to cease from work, and ceasing from working is far more than physical rest, as resting in Christ from the work of trying to save ourselves is its central aspect. We rest in the finished work of Christ. God finished His work of creating on the seventh day, and we cease our working to save ourselves by trusting in Jesus and His finished work on the cross. It was there that Jesus died in our place, His sacrifice atoning for our sin.

Since our own work cannot achieve the covering of our sin, we can only cease from our labor and rest in Christ.

C. "I will give you rest"

The above sentence is found in two places in the Bible. One is in Exodus, and the other is in Matthew.

---

2 The early Church, even in the Book of Acts, substituted Sunday for the Jewish Sabbath and called it the Lord's Day. One reason was that Jesus was raised from the dead on Sunday and also because Christians began to be excluded, or excluded themselves, from the traditional Sabbath observance in the synagogues.

Exodus 33:14 reads, "My presence will go with you, and I will give you rest."

Here the words presence and rest are linked together. The passage is an assurance to Moses that the people of Israel, in their wanderings in the wilderness on their way to the Promised Land, will not be alone but that God would be with them. In the midst of their struggles they will have rest, because God's presence will be with them.

Matthew 11:28 reads, "Come to me, all who labor and are heavy laden, and I will give you rest."

Jesus spoke these words. It is an invitation to come into His presence—"come to me." In our coming to Him and ceasing from our own labor, He will give us rest.

Sabbath and rest have an obvious connection. To rest is to trust that Jesus saves us completely without requiring anything on our part—everything from church membership, baptism, communion, or any other possible good work. This is what is meant when Jesus cried out on the cross, "It is finished" (John 19:30).

D.   Grace and Mercy

These two concepts express our resting in Jesus. It is Jesus who gives us rest. Paul put it this way: "For by grace you have been saved through faith. And this is not your own doing; it is the gift of God, not a result of works, so that no one may boast" (Ephesians 2:8-9).

E.   Joshua versus Jesus[3]

Joshua, Moses' lieutenant, was the person who led the People of Israel through the Jordan River, conquered Jericho, and settled them into what is now the territory or land of Israel. Joshua gave them rest. It was neither permanent nor peace-

---

3   Joshua was Moses' second in command and brought the People of Israel into the Promised Land. His name means "one who saves." Jesus is the same name and means the same thing, probably not a coincidence.

ful but was a period filled with strife and warfare. Well over a millennium later the Romans conquered Israel and occupied it until Jerusalem and the temple were destroyed in AD 70. The writer of Hebrews contrasted Joshua and Jesus in chapter 4, verses 8–10:

> For if Joshua had given them rest, God would not have spoken of another day later on. So then, there remains a Sabbath rest for the people of God, for whoever has entered God's rest has also rested from his works as God did from his.

The rest that Joshua won for Israel was not complete. In Psalm 95 there is clear indication of this. "They shall not enter my rest" (Psalm 95:11). History shows that Israel did not remain in the Promised Land. Modern day Israel is a secular nation without a Temple.

Christians rest in the salvation that Jesus has given and are completely secure in this gift of grace that can never be taken from them.

Lesson Eleven

Peace

To rest in the presence of God is to attain peace. The resting is based upon grace, which comes to us by the election or choosing of God. It is completely God's choice to extend this grace, since we do not deserve it by anything we have done or accomplished. Since we are therefore absolutely incapable of saving ourselves, it is an act of God's mercy to save us.

A.   Peace with God

Perhaps the clearest and simplest expression of the core meaning of peace is found in Romans 5:1:

> Since we have been justified by faith, we have peace with God through our Lord Jesus Christ.

"By faith" needs some explanation. We will think that faith is something we bring to the equation, or to put it another way, we suppose we are responsible for our faith. However, recalling Ephesians 2:8–9 we find that faith itself is a gift of God. If salvation were not a gift there would be no grace; instead we would be acting to earn God's favor.

In addition, "justified" is a word that means God has so acted that it is as though we had never sinned, and will never have sin charged against us again. It contains the truth that all our sin has been removed from us—past, present, and future—and that there is nothing further to make us guilty before a holy and righteous God. How this is, how this works, we do not know.[1] It is one of those mysteries God operates within, and short of being in His presence in heaven, it will always remain a mystery.

Peace is with God and not others. Human conflict is a symptom of not having peace with God. There are two separate and distinct usages of the word "peace" in Scripture. One is absence of conflict and the other refers to the cessation of war that exists between God and us. In Christ, the war has come to an end and we are at peace with God. In the realized kingdom of God, inaugurated at the Second Advent or return of Messiah Jesus, there will also be an end to the conflict between persons, groups, and nations.

We are in the world but not of it, and we experience plenty of warfare and conflict while we sojourn in the world. Jesus put it this way: "I have said these things to you, that in me you may have peace. In the world you will have tribulation. But take heart; I have overcome the world" (John 16:33).

Jesus overcame sin by means of His dying on the cross. Paul put it this way in Colossians 1:19-20:

> For in him all the fullness of God was pleased to dwell, and through him to reconcile to himself all things whether on earth or in heaven, making peace by the

---

1 Bible commentators have reasoned that God covers all our sin at once, since He exists outside of time and space and thus deals with us in a moment, a singular point outside of time that encompasses all of time. 1 John 1:9 teaches that we are to confess our sins on an ongoing basis. Here we encounter one of the many paradoxes found in Scripture.

blood of his cross.

Peace with God is only through Jesus. Jesus died in our place, cleansing us from sin, and it is sin that separates us from God. Once the sin is removed then we can rest in the presence of God—this is our peace. This central biblical truth is well explained by Jesus Himself: "Peace I leave with you; my peace I give to you. Not as the world gives do I give to you. Let not your hearts be troubled, neither let them be afraid" (John 14:27).

Lesson Twelve

Two Messiahs

There is really only one Messiah, who is Jesus, but we see two pictures of the Messiah in Scripture. "Christ" is an English transliteration of the Greek word *Christos*, meaning one anointed by God or set aside and commissioned by God. In Hebrew the same meaning is seen in the word *Mashiach*, from which we get the English word Messiah. Kings of Israel were anointed by prophets, thus identifying them as kings. It is closely akin to the idea of an inauguration.

In the Hebrew Bible, or the Old Testament, we find two pictures of the Messiah or Anointed One, and they are quite different from each other. One may be referred to as "Messiah Son of David," and the other as "Messiah Son of Joseph."

A. Messiah Son of David

David[1] was and is still seen as the greatest king of Israel, whose reign is considered unsurpassed by any subsequent king, even

---

1   David, the son of Jesse of Bethlehem-Ephratah in Judah, was the youngest of eight brothers and two sisters. He was the second and greatest king of Israel.

Solomon his son (the "Wise"). David expanded the actual territory of Israel, defeated her enemies, brought prosperity to the kingdom, and won wide respect for the nation. He was beloved of God.

Prophecies showed that the Messiah would be the offspring of David and would be born in Bethlehem, the city of David (see Micah 5:2). In John 7:42 we read what Jesus' opponents said of Him, "Has not the Scripture said that the Christ comes from the offspring of David?"[2] The support for this comes from, among others, 2 Samuel 7:12-17, 26 and Psalm 89:3-4. There developed, therefore, among the traditions of the people of Israel, an understanding that when the Messiah arrived, He would be like the greatest of Israel's kings and would be a direct descendant of David. This Messiah became known as Messiah Son of David.

B.   Messiah Son of Joseph

This Joseph was the eleventh son of Jacob and the first son of Rachel. He was also his father's favorite son and received from him the famous coat of many colors.[3] His bothers hated him for this and eventually faked his death and sold him to traders who were going to Egypt. There he was sold as a slave, was accused by his master's wife of attempted rape, and thrown into prison. Joseph's story is one of rejection by his own, false accusations, and other cruelties. However, due to his God-given gift to interpret dreams, he became the second most powerful official in Egypt and ended up saving his entire family, including the brothers who had betrayed him, when a severe famine swept through the region.

Joseph became known long before the life and times of Je-

---

2   It was not commonly known during Jesus' ministry where He was born. It was only known that the family of Jesus lived in Nazareth of Galilee, so the argument was that Jesus could not be the Messiah, since he was supposedly born not in Bethlehem but in Nazareth.

3   See Genesis 37:1-4.

sus as the suffering servant of Israel.

Oddly enough, King David, in Psalm 22, wrote of a man's suffering and dying. In fact, the Psalm describes a man dying by crucifixion several centuries prior to any nation or power used crucifixion as a means of execution.

In addition, the prophet Isaiah spoke eloquently in chapters 52 and 53 of someone dying for the sins of the people.

C. Two Messiahs?

Two messiahs were thus in the conversation of Israel, but due to the circumstance of Israel being so often under the yoke of foreign and pagan nations, the hope for a Messiah Son of David predominated. This was certainly evident in the first century AD in the Jewish desire to be free of Roman tyranny. Messiah Son of David was what the people yearned for, and since Jesus' kingdom was not of this world, He was ignored and rejected.

At His first advent Jesus fulfilled the prophecy of the suffering servant, Messiah Son of Joseph. At His second advent Jesus will fulfill the prophecies of the Son of David, the mighty warrior king who will establish an everlasting kingdom.

D. Jesus' first sermon

The sixty-first chapter of Isaiah opens with a long-recognized Messianic passage. It is often titled, "The Year of the LORD's Favor." Jesus quoted it in His first public sermon, which took place in the synagogue at Nazareth, the village where He had been brought up. He visited the synagogue, probably on a Saturday morning. Perhaps by invitation He stood up to read. When the scroll of Isaiah was given to Him, he unrolled it and found the passage where it is written:

> The Spirit of the LORD is upon me, because he has anointed me to proclaim good news to the poor. He has sent me to proclaim liberty to the captives and recovering of sight to the blind, to set at liberty those who are oppressed, to proclaim the year of the LORD's favor.

(Luke 4:18–19)

Jesus then rolled the scroll up and sat down, all while everyone was looking at Him. And He said to them, "Today this Scripture has been fulfilled in your hearing" (Luke 4:21).

Lesson Thirteen

Judgment

One might ask, "Must judgment be a major biblical theme?[1] After all, it is rather negative." My answer must be that, however negative it may be, it is essentially a major aspect of the very nature of God, namely His holiness.

In Genesis 2:15–17 is the first promise of judgment issued by the Creator God:

> The LORD God took the man and put him in the garden of Eden to work it and keep it. And the LORD commanded the man, saying, "You may surely eat of every tree of the garden, but of the tree of the knowledge of good and evil you shall not eat, for in the day that your eat of it you shall surely die."

They did eat, as you know, and although they did not physically die just then, they did experience another and far more consequential death—they were excluded from the presence

---

[1] This topic was touched on in the "Presence" theme, but the theme of judgment needs to be approached in a more direct manner.

of God: "He drove out the man, and at the east of the garden of Eden he placed the cherubim and a flaming sword that turned every way to guard the way to the tree of life" (Genesis 3:24).

God had given His law, it was broken, and judgment followed. Judgment *must* follow the breaking of God's law, since sin cannot stand in the presence of God. Without that judgment—well, it is impossible even to imagine what our world would look like without it.

This is the human story; there is none righteous, no not one. None of us lives in the presence of God, although in Christ we will one day dwell in His presence, which is His garden, His paradise, His heaven. As a guarantee of this He gives us His indwelling Holy Spirit from the moment we are born from above.

A.   Historical Prophetic Drama

The majority of the followers of Jesus will at one time or another struggle with some of the things God commands in the Old Testament. One thinks of God's order to Joshua to slaughter the seven people groups living in the land of Canaan when the Israelites enter the area.

We find the account of this in the Book of Joshua. Moses' lieutenant was to lead the Israelites into a land inhabited by seven tribes—the Canaanites, Hittites, Hivites, Perizzites, Girgashites, Amorites, and Jebusites. Joshua's army was required to completely destroy them, leaving nothing and no one behind, since they were idol worshippers who could and did eventually lead Israel into trouble. (It is a long story, but this is the essential summary.)

The judgment of God came in real time, not at the end of time. Why? My view is that the conquest of Canaan was a historical prophetic drama that graphically displayed God's judgment on sin. This event came centuries before the day of Jesus and the crucifixion when the great judgment of sin took place.

Although this may not satisfy our objections, it is still a way to understand temporal judgment.

B. Jesus and Judgment

Jesus said, "For judgment I came into this world, that those who do not see may see, and those who see may become blind" (John 9:39). How one reacted to Jesus, either accepting or rejecting Him, would be the basis of judgment. Most of the religious leaders of that day did reject Him; Jesus' words were intended to be a wake-up call. This shocking truth is made even more clear in John 5:22–24:

> The Father judges no one, but has given all judgment to the Son, that all may honor the Son, just as they honor the Father. Whoever does not honor the Son does not honor the Father who sent him. Truly, truly, I say to you, whoever hears my word and believes him who sent me has eternal life. He does not come into judgment, but has passed from death to life.

The ministry of Jesus has a great deal then to do with judgment but not merely of the temporal sort; His judgment is eternal in nature.

C. Paul and Judgment

One of the most striking statements about God's judgment is found in Romans 2:5: "But because of your hard and impenitent heart you are storing up wrath for yourself on the day of wrath when God's righteous judgment will be revealed."

Paul points out that God's judgment is "righteous." As utterly holy, God will not and actually cannot tolerate the presence of sin and evil. It must be judged.

The Day of Judgment, a familiar theme in the Old Testament, is found throughout the New Testament as well. Paul, the apostle of both judgment and grace, put it this way in Romans 5:15–16:

> But the free gift is not like the trespass. For if many died through one man's trespass, much more have the grace

of God and the free gift by the grace of that one man Jesus Christ abounded for many. And the free gift is not like the result of that one man's sin. For the judgment following one trespass brought condemnation, but the free gift following many trespasses brought justification.

Paul contrasts what Adam did with what Jesus did. Adam's sin led to death, but Jesus's death led to justification. Indeed, those who are in Christ have had all their sin forgiven, and it is as though they had never sinned at all. He wrote, "Therefore, since we have been justified by faith, we have peace with God through our Lord Jesus Christ" (Romans 5:1).

D. Judgment in Revelation

In the first book of the Bible, Genesis, we see the reason for the necessity of judgment and how it began. In the last book of the Bible we have horrific accounts of that judgment. Over and over, John the Apostle, as revealed to him by Jesus, describes or relates the reality of a final Day of Judgment.

In seven separate visions John sees judgment come at the end of the age. Three of these, the most complete accounts, are those of the seals, the trumpets, and the bowls. Judgment comes upon the unbelieving world. Here is a verse that serves as typical of dozens of such in his book:

> And he said with a loud voice, "Fear God and give him glory, because the hour of his judgment has come, and worship him who made heaven and earth, the sea and the springs of water" (Revelation 14:7).

Toward the conclusion of the Revelation are more complete and detailed passages speaking of the Day of Judgment. One of most startling is Revelation 20:11–15:

> Then I saw a great white throne and him who was seated on it. From his presence earth and sky fled away,

> and no place was found for them. And I saw the dead, great and small, standing before the throne, and books were opened. Then another book was opened, which is the book of life. And the dead were judged by what was written in the books, according to what they had done. And the sea gave up the dead who were in it. Death and Hades gave up the dead who were in them, and they were judged, each one of them, according to what they had done. Then death and Hades were thrown into the lake of fire. And if anyone's name was not found written in the book of life, he was thrown into the lake of fire.

The "books" in the above passage are not likely books as we know them. God is omniscient—all knowing—and He is the cosmic, eternal computer, so to speak, who knows all those who are His children. The code language we find in Revelation is complex to decipher, but the meaning is abundantly clear. There will be a judgment at the end of the age, and it will be final and just.

A note now on the idea that the outcome of judgment depends on what a person has done. We are aware that salvation is by grace and not by works, as explained so clearly in Ephesians 2:8–10. The real work is to believe in Jesus. One day Jesus was asked, "What must we do to be doing the works of God?" His response was, "This is the work of God, that you believe in him whom he has sent." This is John 6:28–29. Then in the same chapter, verse 40, Jesus says, "For this is the will of my Father, that everyone who looks on the Son and believes in him should have eternal life, and I will raise him up on the last day."

In the very last chapter of the Bible we find reference to the very first chapters of the Bible:

> "Blessed are those who wash their robes, so that they may have the right to the tree of life and that they may enter the city by the gates. Outside are the dogs and sorcerers and the sexually immoral and murderers and

idolaters, and everyone who loves and practices falsehood." (Revelation 22:14–15)

Their robes are washed in the blood of Jesus, which means they have been cleansed and forgiven of all sin and can thus be in the presence of God. The "tree of life" hails from Genesis 2:9 and is a historical, prophetic, dramatic symbol of Jesus Himself who, like that tree, gives eternal life.

"Outside" is the place away from the presence of God, where all those whose sin has not been forgiven must stay, since they cannot stand in the presence of a holy God. They are never at rest and have no peace, but are forever kept away from the presence of God.

Lesson Fourteen

Persecution/Triumph of Christ's Church

Spiritual warfare has been waged since the beginning of the history of the universe. It is unknowable whether there was a battle going on prior to the creation of all there is.

What we do know is that there was a rebellion by a powerful and majestic angel directed against the Triune God. The result was that this creature's exalted place in the presence of God was lost forever.

In the third chapter of Genesis is the record of a creature referred to as "the serpent," who was "more crafty than any other beast of the field the LORD God made" (Genesis 3:1). We get a clue to the serpent's identity in 2 Corinthians 11:3: "But I am afraid that as the serpent deceived Eve by his cunning, your thoughts will be led astray from a sincere and pure devotion to Christ." If we need more, we can look to Revelation 12:9: "And the great dragon was thrown down, that ancient serpent, who is called the devil and Satan, the deceiver of the whole world—he was thrown down to the earth, and his angels were thrown down with him."

An exalted angel became the devil, the adversary of God, and took many of his fellow angels with him. And so the war began.[1]

A. The woman, the serpent, and their offspring

Often referred to as the first prophecy in Scripture, Genesis 3:15 is the barest but clearest of outlines for the persecution of and triumph of Christ's Church.

To Satan, the serpent, God spoke these words:

> I will put enmity between you and the woman,
> and between your offspring and her offspring;
> he shall bruise your head,
> and you shall bruise his heel.

God judges the fallen angel when He declares that the offspring of the woman will deliver a death blow to the serpent, and by implication, to his offspring as well.

"Enmity" means conflict, battle, and war, and so it has been from that day to this. "The woman" may certainly be Eve, but is also variously Israel, the chosen people of God, the line of Messiah through Judah, David, and many more. The woman is also the virgin of Isaiah 7:14 and 9:6, who gives birth to Immanuel, "God with us," a child who is called "almighty God." She is then Mary of Nazareth, through whom the ancient prophecy is fulfilled. Immediately upon the birth of the Child the enemy tries to destroy Him through the agency of a jealous and paranoid Herod the Great. Next, at least in the biblical account, we find Satan alone with Jesus in the desert, doing all he can to thwart the mission of the Apostle from God. Only by the overarching will of God does the Passover Lamb go to the cross and shed His blood for the remission of sin.

The serpent was defeated, but he was not through trying to wreak havoc and revenge. The serpent could fight but would

---

[1] Also see Revelation 20:1-3, Isaiah 14:12-15, Ezekiel 28:11-13, 2 Peter 2:4, and Jude 6.

only manage to "bruise his heel." It seems much more than that to us, but in eternity's perspective, it was merely the bruising of the heel.

The woman, already identified progressively as Eve, then Israel who bears the line of the Messiah, then the actual virgin Mary, whose offspring is the Messiah—Immanuel, God with us. Then the offspring is the Church, the Body of Christ, which Jesus established and which becomes the people of God.[2] This battle goes right up to the Day of Judgment, the Second Coming of Jesus Himself.

B.   Jesus and Spiritual Warfare

Jesus knew the wiles of the devil. For forty days alone in the wilderness (see Matthew 4:1–11) Jesus stood upon the revealed truth of Scripture, prevailing against Satan's attempts to tempt Him to scuttle His mission, and when the "devil had ended every temptation he departed from him until an opportune time" (Luke 4:13). One gets the impression that the devil dogged Jesus' tracks throughout His earthly ministry.

Jesus, more aware of the potency of Satan than anyone ever would be, said some very interesting things to the Church about the devil, some of which follow:

> "He was a murderer from the beginning, and has nothing to do with the truth, because there is no truth in him. When he lies, he speaks out of his own character, for he is a liar and the father of lies" (John 8:44).
>
> "Now is the judgment of this world, now will the ruler of this world be cast out" (John 12:31).

---

2   There is a profound distinction between the "visible" and the "invisible" church. The visible church is that which claims to be the church, the visible institution, whether made up of actual Christians or not. The invisible church is made up of only those known to God alone, regardless of denomination or any other manner of designation, who have been born anew or again or from above by the Holy Spirit.

"For false christs and false prophets will arise and perform great signs and wonders, so as to led astray, if possible, even the elect" (Matthew 24:24).

Jesus fully disclosed what His Church would experience; there would be no surprises. In John 16:33 we read, "I have said these things to you, that in me you may have peace. In the world you will have tribulation. But take heart; I have overcome the world."

C. Paul and Spiritual Warfare

Paul also battled the devil during his time. He knew Satan as the "prince of the power of the air" (Ephesians 2:2). The apostle to the Gentiles learned much about spiritual warfare, part of which is found in Ephesians 6:10–12:

> Finally, be strong in the Lord and in the strength of his might. Put on the whole armor of God, that you may be able to stand against the schemes of the devil. For we do not wrestle against flesh and blood, but against the rulers, against the authorities, against the cosmic powers over this present darkness, against the spiritual forces of evil in the heavenly places.

Paul went on to describe the weapons of the Christian's warfare against evil, but of the reality of the battle itself he had no illusions. One of his most profound statements is found in 2 Corinthians 11:13–15, when Paul found it necessary to warn the Corinthian church about those who would bring trouble into their midst:

> For such men are false apostles, deceitful workmen, disguising themselves as apostles of Christ. And no wonder, for even Satan disguises himself as an angel of light. So it is no surprise if his servants also disguise themselves as servants of righteousness. Their end will correspond to their deeds.

The devil would persecute, might win some skirmishes,

but he would fail in the end.[3]

D.   John and Revelation

John, the beloved disciple, spoke of Jesus' ministry in this way: "The reason the Son of God appeared was to destroy the works of the devil" (1 John 3:8). And because of that victory, John could say, "Little children, you are from God and have overcome them, for he who is in you is greater than he who is in the world" (1 John 4:4).

John faced the first empire-wide persecution of the Church, and in the last decade of the first century AD, because of his witness for Christ, he was exiled to the Isle of Patmos off the western coast of the Roman province of Asia, now Turkey. There Jesus revealed to him the reality that persecutions would come to the Church throughout its history, and that they would be severe. Toward the end the Church would actually be overcome. In Revelation 11:7, it was told to John that "the beast that rises from the bottomless pit will make war on them and conquer them and kill them." The "beast" is otherwise known as the antichrist, a front or mask for Satan. Near the time for the return of Jesus at the end of the age and at the time of the Day of Judgment, the beast appears to win the battle but is finally destroyed in hell forever. This tale is told in Revelation 20:7–10.

The serpent has received the death blow already at the cross, and his end is only a matter of time.

As for those who belong to Jesus, we find the following glorious account, and notice the obvious references to the garden of Genesis:

> Then the angel showed me the river of the water of life, bright as crystal, flowing from the throne of God and of

---

[3] For more on the subject of spiritual warfare and how Jesus and His Church cast out demons today visit www.evpbooks.com for my book, *Deliver us from Evil: How Jesus Casts out Demons Today.*

the Lamb through the middle of the street of the city; also, on either side of the river, the tree of life with is twelve kinds of fruit, yielding its fruit each month. The leaves of the tree were for the healing of the nations. No longer will there be anything accursed, but the throne of God and of the Lamb will be in it, and his servants will worship him. They will see his face, and his name will be on their foreheads. And night will be no more. They will need no light of lamp or sun, for the Lord God will be their light, and they will reign forever and ever. (Revelation 22:1–5)

Section I, Continued:
The Basic Lessons

Part 3:
The Church and Christian Life

Lesson Fifteen

The Church

The English word "church" is not actually a translation for the Greek word that is transliterated *ekklesia*.[1] When Jesus said to Peter, "I will build my church" (Matthew 16:18), "church" is *ekklesia*. The word means "called out ones." It also has the idea of a gathering, congregation, or assembly, which is the root idea of the word synagogue.

A. The Visible and the Invisible Church

There is a visible church and an invisible Church. The visible church may be joined. The invisible cannot be joined; rather one must be joined to it by God. Anyone may walk in the front door of the visible church, and is always welcome, but the actual, real, invisible Church is known only to God.

The Church is people, not a building or an institution, although we (perhaps carelessly) refer to a brick and mortar structure as a church. But we know the difference.

---

1 To transliterate is to put equivalent English letters in place of, in this case, the Greek letters. "*ek*" is a preposition meaning out. "*klesia*" is a noun that means call. The root idea is to call out.

B. The Church—the Body of Christ

Christ Jesus is the head of the Church, and the Church is His body.[2] This is a core metaphor used in the New Testament for the Church. Paul wrote, "Christ is the head of the church, his body, and is himself its Savior" (Ephesians 5:23). And then also, "And he is the head of the body, the church. He is the beginning, the firstborn[3] from the dead, that in everything he might be preeminent" (Colossians 1:18).

The nation of Israel, God's people in the Old Testament, was a proto-type of the Church Christ built and which came into its fullness at Pentecost. There are varying views as to when the Church began, everything from Adam and Eve being a "congregation" to Jesus' calling of the twelve disciples. It is clear, however, in Acts 1 and 2, that we see the Church in action.

C. Local and the Universal Church

Upon conversion, the new birth from above, a person is placed into the body of Christ, the Church. This is an act of the Holy Spirit who "baptizes" into the body of Christ. We find this truth in 1 Corinthians 12:12–13:

> For just as the body is one and has many members, and all the members of the body, though many, are one body, so it is with Christ. For in one Spirit we were all baptized into one body—Jews or Gentiles, slaves or free—and all were made to drink of one Spirit.

This is the universal Church. Yet each Christian is to be part of a local church. Most references to church in the New Testament are to local churches. For instance, in 1 Corinthians

---

2   To refer to the Church as the "Body of Christ" is to employ a metaphor that has its origin in Scripture itself. As a human body has different parts, arms, toes, etc., so the individual members of the Church perform different functions.

3   "Firstborn" means head of or ruler over and does not refer to any sort of birthing.

we find Paul saying, "To the church of God that is in Corinth, to those sanctified in Christ Jesus, called to be saints together with all those who in every place call upon the name of our Lord Jesus Christ, both their Lord and ours" (1 Corinthians 1:2).

In the New Testament era, indeed for several centuries, Christians met in each other's homes,[4] or even in caves, groves of trees, or in corners of the Temple in Jerusalem before it was destroyed.

Local churches are comprised of sinners, thus no church is perfect. Some have just been converted and are thus "infants," others are in the toddler stage, others are young children, older children, adolescents, teenagers, young adults, older adults, and elder adults—all spiritually speaking. A church can be a rough and tumble place as people's experiences with sin and the fallen world are being healed. Despite trying times in local churches, Christians will continue to seek out other Christians with whom they can gather for worship and fellowship.

D. The Church and the Kingdom of God

Generally, Christians observe a distinction between the Church and the Kingdom of God, with the latter being those who belong to God in Christ, living or dead. The Church is those who belong to Christ and are presently living.

Jesus is present in the Church and in local churches as well. This is plain from what Jesus Himself said. "For where two or three are gathered in my name, there am I among them" (Matthew 18:20). The context for this verse is church discipline, but the basic principle applies in any case.

E. Membership in the Local Church

Different churches have different requirements for membership. Baptists often require immersion in water, which is part

---

4   Paul cites "house" churches in Romans 16:5, 1 Corinthians 16:19, and Colossians 4:15.

of what gives Baptists their name. This is based on Matthew 28:19–20: "Go therefore and make disciples of all nations, baptizing them in the name of the Father and of the Son and of the Holy Spirit, teaching them to observe all that I have commanded you."

Others, including Baptists, consider a person a member by virtue of his or her presence. Most require baptism; many have a set of classes to attend to acquaint a person with various doctrines, faith policies and positions, and so on. There is considerable variation among churches.

Most churches are small, with a majority under 75 people. There are mega-churches numbering in the thousands of members, often with several campuses in different locations. As mentioned above, there are "house churches," which is a growing trend, but the practice is ancient, going back to the first century of the Christian era.

F. Models of Church Government

Different churches will adopt different forms of governance; these usually fall into either the congregational, episcopal, or eldership (presbyterian) model. Baptists are most often congregational, having a combination of leaders with delegated authority and a democratic element as well. Episcopal is hierarchical in nature, as seen in the Roman Catholic and Anglican/Episcopal Churches. The eldership model, or Presbyterian form of government, is rule by selected or elected elders.

There is biblical precedent for each of these forms of government found in the New Testament. Many churches, in actuality, employ a rough combination of these forms, sometimes evolved over a course of time.[5]

G. Church Leadership

There are several designations for the general officers in the

---

5   Miller Avenue Baptist Church is a combination and an informal one for the most part, of all three of these models.

church. "And he gave the apostles, the prophets, the evangelists, the pastors and teachers, to equip the saints for the work of ministry, for building up the body of Christ" (Ephesians 4:11–12). The apostle, meaning one sent, might be likened to a missionary. The prophet is one who presents the Word of God, in other words, a preacher. The evangelist is one whose focus is the telling of the story of salvation, the Gospel. The pastor/teacher, really one office, cares for the local church through the means of preaching and teaching Scripture.

The terms elder, presbyter, pastor, bishop, overseer are generally synonymous. Also mentioned in the New Testament is the deacon. These do certain tasks, allowing the general officers to focus on the teaching, praying, and preaching. Examine Acts 6:1–7 to see the creation of the position of deacon in the early church. This office was considered to be very important by Paul. Examine 1 Timothy 3 for the qualifications of the officers in the church, including deacons.

H.   Women in the Church

An examination of Joel 2:28–29 shows that women receive gifts of the Spirit. Lists of the gifts of the Spirit are found in 1 Corinthians 12:8–10 and Romans 12:6–8.

The deacon, "Philip the evangelist," had four daughters who "prophesied" (see Acts 21:8–9). There was also Anna, a prophetess (Luke 2:36), and Paul commended women whom he called his fellow workers (see Romans 16:3 and 16:12). And then, Paul asked the Philippian Church to help Euodia and Syntyche, as they had been laboring side by side with him in ministry (see Philippians 4:2–3).

Perhaps the most relevant passage in Scripture that speaks to the issue of women in the church is Galatians 3:28. It reads: "For there is neither Jew nor Greek, there is neither slave nor free, there is neither male nor female, for you are all one in Christ Jesus."

Some churches are adamant that women should not be in

a position of leadership over men in the church. Others disagree and interpret certain passages differently. This issue is best considered a conversation and not a debate, and will be discussed again in section two.

I. The Church in the World

The Church in the world is Christ in the world; the Church is His body, hands, and feet. The Church is in the world but not of it. All who name the name of Christ and are called by Him are the Church, which is the single most important entity on the planet.

Lesson Sixteen

The Christian Ethic

Christians have the highest standard: Jesus Christ. We are to be like Jesus; yet, as we study His life, we find a great gap between Jesus and us. We do grow up into Christ-likeness, incrementally. Despite our struggles, we continue to aim at His perfection.

In both Old and New Testaments we find passages that list attitudes and behaviors to reject and turn away from as well as principles to guide us in our living.

A. The Old Testament's Witness

1. **The Ten Commandments** listed in Exodus 20 and Deuteronomy 5 have stood the test of time and are helpful for us today. Briefly they are as follows:

    - Have no other gods besides the LORD GOD
    - Do not make images of gods in order to worship them
    - Do not take the name of God in vain (as in curses, spells, magic formulas, etc.)

- Remember the Sabbath day to keep it holy (to rest and worship)
- Honor your father and mother
- Do not murder
- Do not commit adultery
- Do not steal
- Do not bear false witness against a neighbor[1]
- Do not covet what belongs to a neighbor

2. **The Two great love commandments in the Hebrew Bible**

    a. Deuteronomy 6:5: You shall love the LORD your God with all your heart and with all your soul and with all your might.

    b. Leviticus 19:18: You shall love your neighbor as yourself.[2]

3. **Abominable Practices**—Deuteronomy 18:9–13

And when you come into the land that the LORD your God is giving you, you shall not learn to follow the abominable practices of those nations. There shall not be found among you anyone who burns his son or his daughter as an offering, anyone who practices divination or tells fortunes or interprets omens, or a sorcerer or a charmer or a medium or a wizard or a necromancer, for whoever does these things is an abomination to the LORD. And because of these abominations the LORD your God is driving them out before you. You shall be blameless before the LORD your God, for these nations,

---

1   The definition of neighbor is quite broad and essentially includes anyone with whom we come into contact. Such is the meaning of neighbor in Jesus' parable of the Good Samaritan (see Luke 10:25–37).

2   Leviticus 19:33–34 commands the Israelites to love strangers living among them. This admonition would be involved in loving one's neighbor as seen in the Parable of the Good Samaritan.

which you are about to dispossess, listen to fortune-tellers and to diviners. But as for you, the Lord your God has not allowed you to do this.

B. The New Testament's Witness

1. The Two Great Commandments—Matthew 22:36–40

"Teacher, which is the great commandment in the Law?" And he said to him, "You shall love the Lord your God with all your heart and with all your soul and with all your mind. This is the great and first commandment. And a second is like it: You shall love your neighbor as yourself. On these two commandments depend all the Law and the Prophets."

2. The Golden Rule—Matthew 7:12 and Luke 6:27–31

"So whatever you wish that others would do to you, do also to them, for this is the Law and the Prophets."

3. Love your enemies—Matthew 5:44 and Luke 23:34

In the Sermon on the Mount, Jesus said:

"You have heard that it was said, 'You shall love your neighbor and hate your enemy.' But I say to you, Love your enemies and pray for those who persecute you, so that you may be sons of your Father who is in heaven.'" (Matthew 5:44)

And then there is Luke 23:34, where Jesus exemplifies this loving your enemies teaching in a most profound way. For those who were responsible for crucifying Him both Roman soldiers, the Jewish leadership, and for us since he died for our sin, He prayed: "Father, forgive them, for they know not what they do."

4. Paul's First List—1 Corinthians 6:9–11

Do you not know that the unrighteous will not inherit the kingdom of God? Do not be deceived: neither the sexually immoral, nor idolaters, not adulterers, not men who practice homosexuality, nor thieves, nor the greedy, nor drunkards, nor revilers, nor swindlers will inherit the kingdom of God. And such were some of you. But you were washed, you were sanctified, you were justified in the name of the Lord Jesus Christ and by the Spirit of our God.

5. **Paul's Second List**—Galatians 5:19–24

Now the works of the flesh are evident: sexual immorality, impurity, sensuality, idolatry, sorcery, enmity, strife, jealousy, fits of anger, rivalries, dissensions, divisions, envy, drunkenness, orgies, and things like these. I warn you, as I warned you before, that those who do such things will not inherit the kingdom of God.

But the fruit of the Spirit is love, joy, peace, patience, kindness, goodness, faithfulness, gentleness, self-control; against such things there is no law. And those who belong to Christ Jesus have crucified the flesh with its passions and desires.

C.   Concluding note:

There are the dos and don'ts in our sacred Text, which are clearly spelled out and are for our benefit. The Creator God knows what is best for us, because He made us the way we are. The breaking of God's laws and principles produces guilt and shame in us—by design. Instead of finding mechanisms to justify our sinful behavior, we are invited to repent, confess, and thus find forgiveness and peace.

Lesson Seventeen

The Christian Life

The greatest of all mysteries and miracles is Christian conversion. In a way that is unexplainable, the Holy Spirit of God convicts us of our sin, shows us the means of our forgiveness in the shed blood of Jesus Christ on the cross, and then opens our hearts and minds to embrace Jesus as Savior and Lord. This is entirely the work of God and is humanly impossible to achieve otherwise.

The most essential issue has been determined now in Christ. We have passed from death into life. Here is how Jesus put it: "Truly, truly, I say to you, whoever hears my word and believes him who sent me has eternal life. He does not come into judgment, but has passed from death to life" (John 5:24). No longer, despite the doubts that are always at war within us, do we concern ourselves about heaven or hell. We no longer wonder what we should do with our lives overall. We are followers of Jesus and the only thing that remains is to bring Him praise and honor in our living. This is our identity and our purpose for living. The details of our living are simply that—important yet details in the grand scheme of things.

A. The Christian Identity

Every Christian has been given a new identity; we are adopted sons and daughters of God by virtue of being born anew though our Lord Jesus Christ. We now belong to the Family of God, the Church.

Our new identity is no longer defined by what we do or have done. "I am a doctor." "I am a minister." "I am a salesperson." "I am a janitor." "I am a failure." "I am a convict," and so on. These phrases may be descriptive, but they do not tell the whole story. Our identity is in Christ. Consider the following passages:

> From now on, therefore, we regard no one according to the flesh. Even though we once regarded Christ according to the flesh, we regard him thus no longer. Therefore, if anyone is in Christ, he is a new creation. The old has passed away; behold the new has come. (2 Corinthians 5:16–17)

> But you are a chosen race, a royal priesthood, a holy nation, a people for his own possession, that you may proclaim the excellencies of him who called you out of darkness into his marvelous light. (1 Peter 2:9)

At Jesus' baptism by John in the Jordan, the Holy Spirit descended upon Jesus, and He heard these words: "This is my beloved Son, with whom I am well pleased" (Matthew 3:17). Part of the spiritual reality of our conversion is that we have been "seated" with Christ in the heavenly places. God has "raised us up with him and seated us with him in the heavenly places in Christ Jesus" (Ephesians 2:6). We are in the Beloved, and this is our identity—we are beloved.

Notice how Scripture refers to us:
- "To all those in Rome who are loved by God and called to be saints" (Romans 1:7).
- "But do not overlook this one fact, beloved, that with

the Lord one day is as a thousand years, and a thousand years as one day" (1 Peter 3:8).
- "Beloved, do not be surprised at the fiery trial when it comes upon you to test you, as though something strange were happening to you" (1 Peter 4:12).
- "Beloved, we are God's children now" (1 John 3:2).
- "Beloved, let us love one another" (1 John 4:7).
- "Beloved, if God so loved us, we also ought to love one another" (1 John 4:11).

Many other passages could be cited, but the point is that we belong to God, warts and all, and nothing can change that. After all, election is not fickle. We are saints, built into the Body of Christ, which is the Church. We are sons and daughters who can never be unborn, and our names are written in the Lamb's Book of Life (see Revelation 13:8 and 21:27). Nothing or no one can erase those names written in stone forever. Nothing or no one can separate us from the love of God in Christ (see Romans 8:31–39).

Our new identity is that we are followers of Jesus—predestined, called, justified, and glorified. That is settled.

B. Doing what Christians Do

Acts 2:42 gives us a concise statement of how the early Christians went about their lives. "And they devoted themselves to the apostles' teaching and fellowship, to the breaking of bread and the prayers."

1. Of primary importance is learning the **apostles' teaching**, which is what they had to say about what Jesus did and said. We do this as we focus on Scripture.[1]

---

[1] Most Christians will want to read the Scripture, the Old and New Testaments. Often this is done in a systematic way. One plan is to read two chapters of the Old Testament, three Psalms, two chapters of a Gospel, and then two chapters from the rest of the New Testament on a daily or weekly basis.

2. **Fellowship** is our gathering together for worship. And fellowship is not so easily done, since we are all yet rather sinful, although we do not want to be. Because we are, we can thus be difficult to get along with. Rather than isolating, Christians work out their differences and learn how to welcome, affirm, forgive, and love one another. The writer of Hebrews said it well: "Let us consider how to stir up one another to love and good works, not neglecting to meet together, as is the habit of some, but encouraging one another" (Hebrews 10:24–25).

The local church is like a refining fire. In order to cooperate, worship together, and serve one another, those things, which are unlovely about us, get worked on and corrected. It is a constant process of growing up in order that we become like Jesus, which is, by the way, what the word Christian means.

Fellowship and breaking of bread are quite similar, so it appears plain that the early church engaged in a double dose of these activities, putting emphasis on being together. The early believers seemed to have spent a lot of time in what is called "table fellowship," and it is likely that the Lord's Supper, Communion, or the Eucharist (all synonyms) was celebrated at the same time.

3. **Prayer** is a major characteristic of Christians, and praying is talking to God—a conversation wherein we talk and God listens. God talks back to us through the Scripture and not in an audible voice as in our conversation with other people. For some, this aspect of the Christian life means a great deal.

4. **Service** in the church is vital. We are meant to work as Paul made clear in Ephesians 2:10: "For we are his workmanship, created in Christ Jesus for good works, which God prepared beforehand, that we should walk in them." The nature of this work and the details of it are not the big issue one might think. It could be anything and any-

where. God is not as concerned about the where and what as He is the mere doing.

5. **Tithing** income and giving offerings were part of the life of Israel. This continued in the early church as well, as evidenced by Acts 2:45: "And they were selling their possessions and belongings and distributing the proceeds to all, as any had need." This pattern was especially necessary at the outset when many of the early converts at Pentecost remained in Jerusalem and needed to be cared for.

Christians throughout the ages have held to free will giving with the tithe or ten percent of one's income as the benchmark. This is both biblical and traditional. Scripture teaches that God loves a cheerful giver, as Paul wrote: "Each one must give as he has made up his mind, not reluctantly or under compulsion, for God loves a cheerful giver" (2 Corinthians 9:7). Each Christian will give what he or she will, and it is freely given.

6. We are called to be **witnesses** to the story of salvation in Jesus. Perhaps Paul, in 2 Corinthians 5:20, put it best: "We are ambassadors for Christ, God making his appeal through us." Herein, for many, is the most exciting aspect of the Christian life. From this work we never retire. Yes, Christians never retire; we simply go on until the end. We never have to concern ourselves with trying to "find ourselves" or acquire meaning and purpose.

It may be said that the Church is the Church as Jesus intended when it is carrying out the mission commands as found in Matthew 28:16–20 and Acts 1:8.

C. Great Differences in the Body of Christ

Being a Christian is not a cookie cutter sort of thing. We do not always see things the same way. There are all kinds of churches and denominations; this has its good and bad points, but more good than bad. There is a church or denomination for everyone. Most of our debating is intramural rather than extramural, meaning that our debates—conversations really—are among the members of the household of God.

Yes, there is false doctrine; yes, there are cults; and no, it is not all the same. We do wrestle with the influence and power of Satan, which is called spiritual warfare. There is a real devil and real demons; we do not close our eyes to this.

One last word: As Christians we refuse to isolate and detach. We are joined to Christ, and we are called to love those in the Church. We learn to forgive and forget, to smooth over our little envies and vanities, and to see Christ in each other.

In the local church, which becomes our spiritual family, is where we live out our lives in service to Christ. To serve in the church is to serve Christ Himself.

D. Spiritual Warfare

"In the world you will have tribulation," Jesus said to his disciples in John 16:33. And so it is. Jesus has overcome the world and all spiritual enemies, but the reality is that there is spiritual warfare that all followers of Jesus engage in to some extent.

Prior to the beginning of Jesus' ministry, Satan attempted to compromise and deceive Jesus. That story is found in Matthew chapter four, often entitled, "The Temptation of Jesus." Jesus countered each temptation by quoting Scripture. Thus we learn from His example how to fight spiritual warfare.

We do not fight alone. In Luke 22:31–32, we see this most clearly when Satan wanted to attack Simon Peter:

> "Simon, Simon, behold, Satan demanded to have you, that he might sift you like wheat, but I have prayed for you that your faith may not fail."

Peter learned, doubtlessly over and over, what the demonic intention is. He wrote:

> Be sober-minded, be watchful. Your adversary the devil

prowls around like a roaring lion, seeking someone to devour. Resist him, firm in your faith, knowing that the same kinds of suffering are being experienced by your brotherhood throughout the world. (1 Peter 5:8–9)

Paul knew about the wiles of the Evil One:

Put on the whole armor of God, that you may be able to stand against the schemes of the devil. For we do not wrestle against flesh and blood, but against the rulers, against the authorities, against the cosmic powers over this present darkness, against the spiritual forces of evil in the heavenly places. (Ephesians 6:10–12)

Paul then goes on to describe the whole armor of God from verses 13 to 18.

Satan, the god of this world, actually battles mightily against the Gospel message by blinding the minds and eyes of those who do not trust in Jesus. (see 2 Corinthians 4:1-4) We see then what a miracle salvation really is.

However horrific Satan and his legions may be, Jesus has defeated them through His death and resurrection. John put it this way: "He who is in you is greater than he who is in the world" (1 John 4:4).

And Christians do not fear the demons and all the power of the devil. It is as Paul instructed his disciple Timothy: "God gave us a spirit not of fear but of power and love and self-control" (2 Timothy 1:7).

And then we have these words from James: "Submit yourselves therefore to God. Resist the devil, and he will flee from you" (James 4:7).

Lesson Eighteen

Church History

Christian history begins with Genesis and the first humans, Adam and Eve. From there, Christian history is also the history of Israel, as Christianity grew out of and is intimately connected to that people and their story—from Abraham, Isaac, and Jacob to Moses, David, Solomon, and the prophets like Isaiah, Zechariah, and all the rest.

A.   From the History of Israel to...

Malachi (whose writing forms the last of the books of the Old Testament canon for Christians) foretold the arrival of a prophet like Elijah who would prepare the way for the Messiah. John the Baptist was that prophet of preparation who showed up some four centuries after Malachi's prophecy. When he saw Jesus of Nazareth coming toward him he shouted out, "Behold, the Lamb of God, who takes away the sin of the world!" (John 1:29). The rest is more specifically Church history.

The Gospels—Matthew, Mark, Luke, and John—describe the life and times of Jesus. Luke's second volume, Acts, outlines some bits of the history of the very early Christian Church, technically starting on Pentecost and proceeding down to about AD 65. Then we turn to the secular historians to tell us the rest of the story.

B.   The History of Christian Thought[1]

Every seminary or Bible college student is required to take church history, some parts of which are intensely interesting, others are boring. But the course is necessary, since we did not arrive in the twenty-first century without considerable background. Every major biblical doctrine has been defined, refined, maligned, twisted, and distorted, until hardly a leaf has been left unturned. To know where we are in terms of what we believe, it helps immensely to see how we got what we have.

Is there one Church? How did the Apostles' Creed, the Nicene Creed, the Heidelberg Catechism, the Canons of Dordt, the Council of Trent, and many other statements of faith and doctrine come about? Who were the Gnostics, the Arians, the Nestorians, and the Moravians? What exactly was the Protestant Reformation? What did Martin Luther do?

Oh, the list goes on. Where did Baptists come from? Who were the Puritans? What about the Quakers, Mormons, Jehovah's Witnesses, and Unitarians? What about Arminianism and Calvinism, two distinct but also similar theologies that all religious constructs fall into one way or the other? Who, where, when, and how—big questions with big answers.

It is not possible here to do more than hopefully arouse curiosity about all the rich history that has gone before. How enlightening to read about Justin Martyr, Ignatius, Tertullian, Origen, Augustine, Jerome, Benedict, Anthony, Aquinas, Luther, Calvin, and so many more. The lives of St. Francis of Assisi, John Knox, John Wesley, George Whitefield, Jonathan Edwards, and Charles Haddon Spurgeon have so much to teach

---

1   This is the title of an excellent book on church history by Jonathan Hill, published by InterVarsity Press in 2003.

and thrill us. These are the big names, and there are so many more to whom we owe so much.

Please take this as an invitation to dig deeper, and when you do, the result will be a far more settled understanding of where the Church is now. It is akin to knowing one's family history, both good and bad. Church history is our history.

Section 2:
Debates and Conversations

Part 1:
Extramural Debates

Extramural Debates: Introduction

Times are changing, but that's not new. The rapid and radical growth of technology, tumult among nations, economic uncertainty, political crises, and more have accelerated or ratcheted up stress levels across the board. And, of course, Christians also have their battles to wage.

By extramural I mean debates that Christians have with non-Christians. It must be acknowledged that some of these debates, especially the fourth one dealing with same-sex marriage, may be considered a cross-over debate, in that some who identify themselves as Christians may be on the pro side of the same-sex debate. However, the issue seems to me to rest on the nature of creation, the intent of the Creator, and the plain word of Scripture. Thus, I see same-sex marriage as extramural.

Christian churches are affected by the winds of culture, and in America presently there is increasing pressure to be tolerant, inclusive, and diverse. One result is what can fittingly be called syncretism, which is the adoption of the ethic and morals of the majority, even when it flies in the face of traditional biblical understanding. Therefore, Christians end up embracing behavior and theological concepts that are aberrant and are in error from a biblical perspective as traditionally understood by all branches of the Christian Church.

In this second section of Christian Basics I will list and briefly comment on four extramural debates, those biblical doctrines that are central to Christianity and set Christianity apart from all other world religions. The fundamental theology found in section one is assumed as the underlying foundation for section two. For instance, the nature of the Triune God has already been presented and will not be reiterated in section two; it is understood. Next come the conversations that are mostly, but not entirely, intramural in nature.

Debate One

The Exclusivity of Jesus

This issue must head the list, since it is the fundamental doctrine, and if it were abandoned, it would render all other issues virtually meaningless.

In John 14:6 Jesus said, "I am the way, and the truth, and the life. No one comes to the Father except through me." He is the way, truth, and life, because He is Emmanuel, God with us—both fully God and fully man.

Only in Jesus and His cross is there salvation. Without this central biblical doctrine Christianity may as well be just another option in the spiritual market place.

Paul expressed the same in Colossians 1:15–20:[1]

> He is the image of the invisible God, the firstborn of all creation. For by him all things were created, in heaven and on earth, visible and invisible, whether thrones or dominions or rulers or authorities—all things were created through him and for him. And he is before all things, and in him all things hold together. And he is

---

1 Also see John 1:1-18, Philippians 2:1-11, and Hebrews 1:1-4.

the head of the body, the church. He is the beginning, the firstborn from the dead, that in everything he might be preeminent. For in him all the fullness of God was pleased to dwell, and through him to reconcile to himself all things, whether on earth, or in heaven, making peace by the blood of his cross.

For biblical and historically oriented Christians the key to identifying heresy has to do with the person and work of Christ. The Scripture is abundantly clear: He is both God and man,[2] and thus His death, or sacrifice on the cross, is sufficient to cleanse from all sin and restore a person to a right relationship with God.

The exclusive claim made by Jesus and for Him in Scripture relegates all other gods and goddesses to something other, something less, something fictional—idolatry at best. Those not committed to Scripture and historic Christian theology will find their attempts to achieve inclusiveness thwarted and resisted. This debate has been and will continue to be a battle ground that is marked by a broad line drawn in the sand.

This argument over the exclusiveness of Jesus has been waged from the very beginning of the Christian era. The actual but invisible and true Christian Church will not retreat on this point.

---

2   The person of Jesus Christ is paradoxical in that it is impossible to reconcile the fact that He is both God and man at the same time. The idea is beyond human ability to resolve into something comfortable and logical. Biblical Christianity does not make an attempt at resolving the apparent conflict.

Debate Two

The Authority of Scripture

Since it is from the Scripture that we learn who Jesus is, a struggle over the Bible's authority naturally follows.

A case in point: Genesis through Chronicles[1] (for the Jewish people) or Genesis through Revelation (for Christian people) reveals that the Messiah is deity. This is evident from passages like Isaiah 7:14 and 9:6. First 7:14: "Therefore the Lord himself will give you a sign. Behold, the virgin shall conceive and bear a son, and shall call his name Immanuel."[2] Then 9:6: "For to us a child is born, to us a son is given; and the government shall be upon his shoulder, and his name shall be called Wonderful Counselor, Mighty God, Everlasting Father, Prince of Peace."[3]

---

1 In the Hebrew Bible, Chronicles is the last book while in most Christian Bibles Malachi ends the Old Testament section of the Bible.

2 Immanuel, sometimes spelled Emmanuel, means "God with us." The ending of the word "el" is a Hebrew word for God.

3 "Son," when applied to Messiah Jesus, does not imply that Jesus is a literal offspring of God the Creator, as though something akin to sexual intercourse was involved. The terms Son of God and Son of Man refer to

These two passages from Isaiah and others from the Hebrew Bible confirm that the Messiah is deity. The New Testament writers clearly proclaim that Jesus was and is that Messiah. The Messiah is God, and Jesus was and is Messiah. Clear enough. It is easy to see why the Bible is attacked as being flawed or even the result of intrigue or conspiracy. Such claims, however, have no historical relevance and only add to the glut of poor fiction.

Here again is a cornerstone argument that will not go away. Battles for and against the Bible will continue to be waged right up to the very end of history.

The Bible is another example of paradox; it springs both from the hand of man and the revelation and will of God. In it, we also see the person of Jesus as both God and man at once, a paradox that will stand and will not be resolved by the mind of humans.

With its seamless web of testimony, from Genesis to Revelation, and despite the seeming contradictions and the evidences of the human hand, yet by the power of the Holy Spirit, the Bible is a battle-tested strong shield and sword.

Ultimately, the belief that the Bible is the inspired Word of God is based on faith not fact. The Bible cannot insist that it is itself inspired, which constitutes a circular argument. Like so much of what we hold to be true, we are looking at a faith position. Paul speaks to this in 1 Corinthians 1:18 and 2:14:

> For the word of the cross is folly to those who are perishing, but to us who are being saved it is the power of God. (1 Corinthians 1:18)

> The natural person does not accept the things of the Spirit of God, for they are folly to him, and he is not able to understand them because they are spiritually dis-

---

Jesus being the Messiah, and this usage is derived from the Old Testament and was current during the earthly ministry of Jesus.

cerned. (1 Corinthians 2:14)

The Bible becomes for the reader and doer of the Word the whole truth from God. It verifies itself over time; it authenticates itself through a powerful and inner witness of the Holy Spirit. It is fascinating how this works, but that it does has been corroborated by millions of Christians over the centuries.

Debate Three

Heaven and Hell

There is a heaven and a hell, not merely a heaven and a nothing.

Atheists do not engage in this debate, because they deny both heaven and hell. Agnostics don't get stirred up either, except in times of crisis. Within the broad Christian community is where the argument may be heard.

Aside from many passages about hell in Scripture, here are places where Jesus Himself talked about an actual hell: Matthew 5:29, 10:28, 18:9, 23:15, 23:33; Mark 9:23; and Luke 12:5. Whether hell is a place or something beyond description, no one knows. However, it is undeniable that, biblically speaking, it is a complete and forever separation from the Triune God.

As a long time pastor I have often sincerely wished that hell was not a reality. I have deceased loved ones who totally rejected anything Christian, and this will always trouble me. But to hold out for a heaven and no hell is only wishful thinking. I would be better off denying both rather than just the unpleasant part. But I cannot; I will not.

The volume and tempo of the argument over hell is increasing, because it connects with the first two debates, the exclusiveness of Jesus and the authority of the Bible. When the culture objects that Christians condemn others to hell if they don't believe in Jesus, and when the gathering army of opposition calls out that this is unacceptable arrogance without the slightest hint of being tolerant and diverse, who can stand the heat?

The argument for tolerance, diversity, and inclusiveness often is anchored by an appeal to the faithful sincerity of adherents to other world religions. Isn't it enough to be sincere? is a question not easily answered even for many Christians.

Some will stand and refuse to retreat, choosing to face the arrows of the enemy. There will be casualties, some will go AWOL, but the man or woman of God, properly equipped with the armor of God, will stand.

Hell will not go away just because it is ugly and repulsive. This largest of barricades will not be overcome despite our fondest wishes.

Debate Four

Same-Sex Marriage

After completing an early draft of this topic, I submitted it to a class of adult Christians for their consideration. Several thought this subject did not belong in the debate but in the conversation section. I accepted the opinion that it could go either way. I still hope it could be a conversation, but many view this particular issue to be a most serious and defining issue amongst Christians.

A.   Five reasons to consider this issue a debate rather than a conversation:

1. To consider homosexuality to be aberrant and wrong is not unique to Christianity; in fact, Judaism, Islam, Hinduism, Buddhism, Baha'i, and others view homosexual behavior similarly. Certainly persons in every and any particular religion will have varying ideas, but core belief for these groups is settled.

2. This issue touches the very heart of God's creation and the nature of human beings. God, scripturally speaking,

meant for heterosexuality to be the norm. And in many passages, homosexuality is presented as an abomination. It fits into the category of "fornication," usually translated "sexual immorality" and refers to any sexuality outside of a man-woman marriage, and such is declared evil by Jesus in Mark 7:20–23:

> And he said, "What comes out of a person is what defiles him. For from within, out of the heart of man, come evil thoughts, sexual immorality, theft, murder, adultery, coveting, wickedness, deceit, sensuality, envy, slander, pride, foolishness. All these evil things come from within, and they defile a person."

Paul's position is also clear; he states in 1 Corinthians 6:9 that those who practice homosexuality will not inherit the kingdom of God:

> Do you not know that the unrighteous will not inherit the kingdom of God? Do not be deceived: neither the sexually immoral, nor idolaters, not adulterers, not men who practice homosexuality, nor thieves, nor the greedy, nor drunkards, nor revilers, nor swindlers will inherit the kingdom of God.

An approval of same-sex marriage comes very close to a denial of the Lordship and deity of Jesus Christ and is also a rejection of the authority of Scripture. Therefore, homosexuality is not a peripheral issue; it lies at its heart against the purpose of God in creation as revealed in the Bible.

3. Those Christian denominations and churches that have opted to approve of homosexuality, in one way or another, do not seem to be committed to a historical doctrinal orthodoxy. This may seem judgmental on my part, and I cannot possibly go about documenting sources to support my statement, but it is still an informed and reality-oriented conclusion. It may well fit the proverbial

"slippery slope" argument posed by many Christian apologists to warn of the decline away from biblical doctrine when certain liberties are taken. My suspicion is that those who promote this currently popular political/social agenda have a weakened, if not absent, commitment to proclaiming the Gospel of Jesus Christ. They have, at least, shifted priorities. Salvation, the difference between an eternity in heaven or hell, has taken a back seat to assuring homosexuals that they are perfectly good and normal.

4. There is apparent in the conversation about same-sex marriage a failure to account for the dramatic impact of the Fall. I am referring to the rebellion against God as recorded in the opening chapters of Genesis. In chapter three of Genesis we find a horrific judgment pronounced by the Creator on the kind of life humans would experience thereafter. All life is affected and that includes human sexuality. Prior to that Fall, Adam and Eve were naked and without guilt or shame. Once the law breaking occurred, Adam and Eve hid from God and noticed they were naked. Innocence was gone, and guilt began to work its twisted course. Nothing much has changed from that over the course of time.

5. Marriage is a historical, dramatic, prophetic depiction of Christ and the Church. Jesus Christ is the bridegroom and the Church is the bride. Christ is in the Church and the Church is united to Christ. Marriage is therefore a living and actual portrayal of the ultimate intention of God, the one flesh union lived out in the world and pointing beyond it to eternal life lived out in the presence of God.

Same-sex marriage, whether a debate or a conversation, will not go away, but will be with us for the long haul. The bottom line is that support for same-sex marriage is basically an acceptance of homosexuality.

Same-sex marriage is the current hot button facing Christians. It is the front line in a battle that could result in the closest we might get to a real spiritual civil war. There is keen pressure to be tolerant and diverse and approve same-sex marriage, including within the evangelical wing of the Church. The struggle for gay rights is cast as something similar to the civil rights movement of the 1960s; this is a false identification in my view. The link between the two—civil rights and an equality for homosexuals that includes legalizing gay marriage—is artificial.

Homosexuality is the topic here. It is not merely a case of wanting to see every person have equality. There is a larger issue that every culture must first confront: What is acceptable sexual behavior and practice? Can a person be equal if their sexual preferences are rejected as abnormal? Are there some forms of sexuality that humans can engage in that are not to be encouraged? The biblical answer is, Yes!

To most it is clear that sex between various combinations, such as a parent and child, adults with young boys or girls, a person and an animal, and sex with close relatives, are completely outside normal limits.[1] To others the prohibitions are not so clear. A secular society, especially one that values separation of church and state, may not rely upon a religious or spiritual document to be the arbiter of what is objectionable. Culturally speaking, there is little or no authority to which to appeal in regard to same-sex practice and by extension same-sex marriage.

It is therefore clear why the question of authority is an extramural debate that comes before this one. If there is no

---

1   Biblical passages that speak to the issue are Leviticus 18:22, 20:13; Mark 7:21; Romans 1:18–25; 1 Corinthians 6:9–10; and 1 Timothy 1:9–10. Note: the word "fornication" refers to sex outside of marriage, whatever form it might take.

biblical authority, then to what can we appeal? Not much, especially in a court of law. If public opinion is the standard, then the loudest voices will prevail, and a minority can eventually change even the U.S. Constitution. The polls actually show wide variations in opinion, and, as previously stated, there is growing support for same-sex marriage in the evangelical Christian camp.

What happens if the effort to maintain one man/one woman marriage is lost? And it is likely to be lost, sooner or later. Little by little, state-by-state, same-sex marriage will become the law of the land. The Christian community may not withstand the cultural onslaught. Certainly not all will go along, and there may be civil disobedience displayed in various ways by those faithful to the biblical worldview. It is right here with same-sex marriage where the Christian-oriented civil war will be most evident.

Will this be a line drawn in the sand? Will this issue highlight what is and what is not truly Christian? I think it easily could.

When asked how I know homosexual behavior is deviant, I only appeal to Genesis chapters one, two, and three, then to Romans 1:18–25. Then I say, "Read these passages and make up your own mind." Christians will not be concerned about what the culture says about homosexuality. Many people groups and entire nations have accepted it to one degree or another. That is history. But, from a biblical point of view, is it normal, good, and acceptable, and should it therefore be approved and normalized? It will certainly take courage to stand and present biblical arguments on this front.

One last little point is worth noting: surveys measuring the growing acceptance of same-sex marriage discovered that people's attitudes changed from disapproval to approval if they personally know a homosexual. It is similar to what happens to a person who has loved ones who died and were not followers of Jesus; they were reluctant to believe in that eternal bad place, thinking that holding to such a belief was tantamount to sending them there.

During my thirty years as a volunteer at San Quentin Prison, members of the baseball teams I managed included serial rapists, pedophiles, and a host of murderers, not to mention drug dealers, thieves, and various sorts of other felons. Some of these men were very fine people, especially after years of hard work to improve themselves. This experience has not caused me to change my mind about the crimes these men committed. I am acquainted with a number of homosexuals, and some are actively practicing homosexuality. And they know me well enough that they do not imagine I have changed my mind about the sinfulness of homosexual behavior. If, when we are together, the topic does come up, my stance remains thoroughly biblical. Certainly my view may become a minority one, but it is valid nevertheless.

Section 2, Continued:

Debates and Conversations

Part 2:

Intramural Conversations

Intramural Conversations: Introduction

One or two of the conversations I cite may be thought by some to belong in the debates section. This is itself debatable. Christians differ among themselves, which is normal and healthy. Probably no two Christians agree on everything; sometimes I don't agree with myself and hold open the option of changing my mind. In regard to what follows, I have held different views on every single one of what I am referring to as intramural conversations. Not so, however, with the extramural debates; my position on these have remained static once I worked through the issues many years ago.

The conversations are not listed in order of importance but are instead alphabetized, because it is not clear what their relative weight is, and they will be thought of differently by different Christians. Some readers will be disappointed at the brevity of the discussions; certainly each deserve far more than what is presented here, but at least the conversations have begun.

Conversation One

Abortion

Abortion is repugnant to most, Christians and non-Christians alike. It is, on the other hand, tolerated by many, meaningless to some, or even simply an acceptable form of birth control to others.

A significant portion of the Christian community is strongly opposed to abortion for any reason; for some it is okay in instances where the mother's life is in jeopardy. Some would criminalize it under most circumstances, others object to it but not to the point of making it a part of the criminal code book. Some favor limits be placed on the practice in terms of what stage of pregnancy is allowable, and there are other issues as well.

Abortion is largely an intramural conversation. For many, on both sides of the issue, it is a captivating issue, even an all-consuming obsession. Some see abortion as murder and thus it is a major issue; a biblical case can be made for this position.

My personal pastoral concern is for women who have experienced abortion, but also for the fathers and even those who perform the abortions. The loss and the traumatic nature of the procedure impact all involved spiritually and emotionally, not to mention physically, and for years to come.

A debate or a conversation? In my view it is a conversation in spite of its polarizing capacity. However, the heart and Gospel of biblical Christianity is not at stake.

Conversation Two

Baptism and The Lord's Supper

Baptism and the Lord's Supper are seen very differently from one Christian denomination to another in terms of what is imparted through them spiritually.

A. **Ordinance or Sacrament?**

1. "Ordinance" means that followers of Jesus are instructed to observe these as a remembrance of what Christ did in his death, burial, and resurrection, which are central to the grounds and basis of our salvation but are not required to be performed to achieve salvation.

2. "Sacrament" embodies the idea that these are necessary for salvation, especially baptism. Here baptism washes away the original sin resulting from the Fall of Adam and Eve and unites a person to the Church by means of a covenant or agreement. It may also convey salvation to the one baptized. Note one nuance: the sacraments do not have saving value but help to convey grace and faith.

B. **First, a look at baptism.**

Jesus was baptized by John the Baptist, and He instructed His disciples to baptize those who became His followers (see Matthew 28:16–20). The 3,000 converted on the Day of Pentecost were baptized that same day (see Acts 2:41); Philip baptized those who were converted under his ministry (see Acts 8:9–13, 34–38); Paul was baptized upon his conversion (see Acts 9:18); Peter baptized those converted under his ministry (see Acts 44–48); and Paul did likewise (see Acts 16:11–15, 25–34). There is more, but this will suffice.

We are baptized, because Jesus intended that we do so, and the early Church continued the practice.

The method of baptism varies. The word itself, derived from the Greek New Testament, means to plunge under, to dunk, or to immerse. Baptists dunk to portray the death, burial, and resurrection of Jesus. It is at once identification with Jesus, a proclamation of the essential Gospel story, and an act of obedience.

Others sprinkle with water or pour water on the head. I have, due to varying circumstances, done both of these. While neither is likely the method employed by John the Baptist or the Apostles, for the baptized person it may be very meaningful. We must be wary of drifting into magical thinking by insisting that the methodology must be perfectly maintained or the act has no potency.

C.   Second, a look at the Lord's Supper.

Communion, Eucharist, Mass—these are terms that mean the same as Lord's Supper. It is a celebration, even re-enactment, of the Passover Meal that Jesus took with His disciples the night He was betrayed. The institution of the Lord's Supper is found in Matthew 26:26–29, Mark 14:22–25, and Luke 22:14–23. (There is no account of the Lord's Supper in John's Gospel.) Here now is Matthew's version:

> Now as they were eating, Jesus took bread, and after blessing it broke it and gave it to the disciples, and said,

"Take, eat; this is my body." And he took a cup, and when he had given thanks he gave it to them, saying, "Drink of it, all of you, for this is my blood of the covenant, which is poured out for many for the forgiveness of sins. I tell you I will not drink again of this fruit of the vine until that day when I drink it new with you in my Father's kingdom."

(Before proceeding let it be noted that the "blessing" of the bread is not a magical formula that makes the bread into something other than bread. Rather, it is thanking God for His provision and grace as we more clearly see in the phrase "giving thanks" with Jesus' introduction of the cup.)

In Luke's account, Jesus states, "Do this in remembrance of me" (Luke 22:19). Paul uses this same concept in 1 Corinthians chapter 11:23–26:

> For I received from the Lord what I also delivered to you, that the Lord Jesus on the night when he was betrayed took bread, and when he had given thanks, he broke it, and said, "This is my body which is for you. Do this in remembrance of me." In the same way also he took the cup, after supper, saying, "This cup is the new covenant in my blood. Do this, as often as you drink it, in remembrance of me." For as often as you eat this bread and drink the cup, you proclaim the Lord's death until he comes.

Over the centuries, especially when people did not have access to written accounts of the Bible, observing the Lord's Supper was a visual Gospel presentation that covered the basics of our Faith: the death, burial, and resurrection of Jesus Christ.

How often should the Lord's Supper be observed? Some Christians do it once a year and usually on Passover, some quarterly, some monthly, and some weekly. "Let each one make up his or her mind" works.

Conversation Three

Church Government

This is almost a non-issue with most people, Christian and non-Christian alike, yet historically speaking, there are some interesting aspects to the subject that are somewhat troublesome even at the present time. And it must be acknowledged that some believe there is only one truly biblical form of church government.

A. Three Basic Forms of Church Governance Found in Scripture

1. Congregational, means governance by the congregation, via a democratic-like model. Baptists subscribe to this model along with a number of other Christian denominations.

2. Episcopal, is a top down form of government with a hierarchical style of leadership. The Roman Catholic Church, Eastern Orthodox, Anglican/Episcopal Church, Methodists, and others adhere to this form.

3. Presbyterian, the third model, is rule by selected elders.

Presbyterian churches and Reformed denominations fall into this category.

B.   All of the Above.

My first pastorate was of a Southern Baptist Church, and although it was supposed to be democratic in a one-member, one-vote style, in reality the deacons made all the decisions. So it was actually a mix of congregational and presbyterian. My second pastorate was designed from the outset to be presbyterian, with the congregation selecting the leaders, but in fact the leaders were largely selected by the senior pastor in the early days (me), then as time went on, by existing elders. Now in my third and last pastorate, our form of government is best described as pastor-led with a mixture of congregational and presbyterian elements involved. This amalgamation is not that unusual, and I suspect it would be difficult to find a church of whatever denomination adhering purely to one form.

C.   An abbreviated examination of organizational styles found in Scripture.

1. Old Testament

Starting with Moses in the mid-second millennium BC, Moses sits at the top and governs according to the Law given at Mt. Sinai. Later on, through the intervention of Jethro, Moses' father-in-law, judges and administrators are appointed by Moses, and the responsibility of ruling is spread out.

After Moses there was a period when God selected and empowered judges over the Israelites, like Deborah and Samson. How this functioned in real time is unclear; in the Book of Judges, it simply says that God raised up certain persons to lead the people. Toward the end of the first millennium B.C. the people of Israel demanded a king like the nations around them. God obliged, and beginning with Saul, the kings of Israel acted like the kings of their numerous and small city-state neighbors. At various points, prophets like Elijah were sent to draw Israel back to the basic understanding that the LORD God was their true King.

2. Transition to New Testament Times

For a large portion of the history of Israel conquering foreign powers ruled over it instead of an Israelite king, priest, or prophet, beginning with Assyria, then Babylon, Greece, Egypt, Syria, and finally Rome. It was under the emperor Tiberius that Jesus walked the land. When Paul wrote Romans 13 containing an injunction to obey the leaders of the land, Nero was the emperor.

The early church seems to have been a mix of congregational, episcopal, and presbyterian models. Jesus appointed the Twelve, and Judas' loss motivated the very primitive church to replace him. Owing to Peter's directive (Acts 1:12-26) the congregation selected two men who could replace Judas, and by lot one was chosen. Then, shortly thereafter, there was a need for administrative types or servants to help the apostles with mundane chores. Seven "deacons" were put forward by the congregation at the request of the Twelve (see Acts 6:1-6).

By Acts chapter 15, about AD 50, a council was convened at Jerusalem to resolve crucial issues. There both apostles and elders acted in some kind of shared authority. The head of the church seems to have been James, the half brother of Jesus (see Acts 15:1-21). After what was probably a considerable discussion, this Council at Jerusalem ended with a decision, voiced by James. Luke, the author of Acts, records the actual decision: "Therefore my judgment is," and then James delivers the details of his decision. To what extent he expressed the opinion of the majority of the apostles, elders, and wider congregation is unknown. But at minimum there is a combining of the three major forms of government under discussion.

Just a little more on the subject: In Ephesians 4:11 Paul lists apostles, prophets, evangelists, pastors and teachers—probably four offices, as pastors and teachers seem to be one grammatically—to be church leaders. Their responsibility was to equip the members of churches for service, not to function as ruling authorities. Then in 1 Corinthians 12:27–30, Paul gives an expanded list of leaders: "And God has appointed in the church first apostles, second prophets, third teachers, then miracles, then gifts of healing, helping, administrating, and various kinds of tongues" (1 Corinthians 12:28). The naming of the "offices" does not clear things up much, since this could belong to any of the three forms of governance or any combination of the three.

D.   Is one model the correct one?

It does not seem valuable to pronounce that any one form of government is closer to the biblical practice than any other. Of greater consequence is the relationship between the church and secular government.

Paul's view puts things into perspective: "Let every person be subject to the governing authorities. For there is no authority except from God, and those that exist have been instituted by God" (Romans 13:1). This is not to suggest that every vile, corrupt, and murderous politician is put in place by the express will of God, but that law and order, not chaos and anarchy, is preferable.

The separation of church and state derives from this biblical principle. The Church will conduct its own discipline, and how this is done is elusive at best, but certainly the Church does not prosecute murder, theft, and so on. It may act in areas such as jealousy, envy, pride, and the list goes on, but there is a separation, unlike other religions, such as Islam's Sharia Law standard.

Church governments within a single church may change over time. At the outset the government may be more top down and then morph later into something else. Whatever form of government a church has, from the leaders to new members, all must see that Jesus is the head of the Church, both universal and local. All who exercise authority do so as servants. Due to our fallen nature, however, there is always the temptation to hold on to power, and thus a certain corruption will set in. Perhaps it is best that a church function with a certain balance of all three of the forms of governance as detected in Scripture.

Conversation Four

Divorce and Remarriage

Divorce is something to avoid, if at all possible, and few would argue this.

A. Christians and Divorce

Most Christians recognize that some divorces are necessary, while others are adamant that divorce is unacceptable for any reason. The differences within the Christian community are rather startling, and I have found that some think divorce is catching like a disease. Some say that accepting divorce and remarriage is like the proverbial slippery slope, which once you start slipping it may be a long slide. Most Christians agree it is important to be faithful to a biblical agenda.

Extreme reactions to divorce and remarriage can get ugly, as divorced people are often stigmatized or even shunned. Yet statistics show that half the marriages in America, for instance, end in divorce. It would be hoped that restoration, reconciliation, and the application of a merciful grace would be at the top of the agenda. Such is more often found in what many consider "liberal" churches, but not always so.

I have experienced divorce and remarriage, both while a pastor. The result was more than unpleasant for all involved. Even after many years, there are still repercussions. As a result, I have wrestled with this subject intensely. Uppermost for me was the question as to whether a person, even a pastor, could be restored and accepted once again into Christian ministry, biblically speaking. Reaction from many pastors was simple: No was the answer; he could not re-enter ministry, especially if such a person remarried. But thankfully there were other answers. It is not an issue of whether divorce is wrong—it is; the issue is whether it is some form of unforgiveable sin or one that disqualifies one from church leadership or even fellowship. After more than four decades as a pastor I have seen worse sins than divorce and/or remarriage. How deadly are the sins of pride, envy, greed, jealousy, and the list goes on and on, and these are rarely ever dealt with. Church discipline can be quite myopic.

B.   God and Divorce

Divorce is not God's will. The divine intention is that a marriage endures unto death. We are clear on this point, and it is also clear that we are not to sin at all but are to be perfect as God Himself is perfect. However, we have a fallen nature and live in a fallen world. Although we are new creatures in Christ, we are not yet in our resurrection bodies in the presence of God, and we face severe spiritual warfare. Many battles are lost along the way.

It is without question that Moses allowed for divorce, as did Jesus and Paul. Each upheld the original intent of God that there should be no divorce, yet they understood the "hardness of heart" of human beings. Therefore, divorce would exist—for the right or wrong reasons. What then? And it is here that the Christian community is divided.

C. Remarriage

The subject of remarriage for the Christian is even more troublesome than divorce. Remarriage is considered by some to be ongoing adultery, a second "one flesh," thus contrary to the express purpose of God.

But then, it can be argued that God did not intend for there to be lying, stealing, envy, jealousy, pride, and so on. Once committed, is the thief always a thief, a liar always a liar, the prideful person always condemned? If so, we are each guilty and might as well abandon hope.

Must divorced Christians then remain unmarried? Oddly, this becomes the larger issue and the flash point of contention. Some say divorcees must remain unmarried, while others hold to the repenting of the sin of divorce and the possibility of remarriage.

Does the blood of Jesus wash away all sin, past, present, and future, or only those sins committed prior to the Christian's justification? Can salvation be lost if he or she experiences divorce? Why did the Apostle John write and to Christians: "If we confess our sins, he is faithful and just to forgive us our sins and to cleanse us from all unrighteousness" (1 John 1:9).

D. Grace versus Works?

Admittedly one's view of conversion and salvation is at the heart of it. Those who rely on "works" and thus the possibility of losing one's salvation will be at odds with those who rely on the mercy and grace of God with good works following. Certainly grace is not a cover for or a license to sin, but if our sinning overcomes God's free grace in Christ, heaven will be largely unpopulated.

Divorce and remarriage—a major debate or a conversation? So far, a majority of Christians have agreed to disagree on this issue, making it a conversation, however hotly contested.

Conversation Five

Ecumenism

Here the issue is whether a Christian may cooperate with, fellowship with, or have any connection with those who do not hold to a particular confession of faith.

In 1986, a year after becoming pastor of Miller Avenue Baptist Church in Mill Valley, I felt that it would be good to establish a fellowship of local pastors. Now in 2015, at least four of the churches continue to hold a joint Good Friday Service. It has been a great experience all the way along. But some say I violated the principle of secondary separation, that is, a requirement to refuse association with anyone who was either in sin or holding to "false" doctrine. After examining the issue, I concluded that if we carried the practice of secondary separation to its obvious extreme, each of us would eventually be all alone.

I am a Baptist (a Protestant denomination) by conviction, yet I regularly work with and have fellowship with almost everyone who identifies themselves as Christian, including other Protestants, Pentecostals, Catholics, Eastern Orthodox, and some who claim to be none of the above. I must admit to having drawn the line at one point on what is often termed "inter-faith" gatherings. After involving myself in Marin County's inter-faith group, I found I was uncomfortable having to accept and at least tacitly approve of the practices and doctrines of weird and wildly non-Christian (really anti-Christian) religions like Wicca and shamanism. However, I have discovered that engagement with those of other faiths has given me a ministry I would not have had otherwise and with good fruit coming as a result of my involvement. However, I know that most evangelicals are skeptical of such organizations.

At one point in my life I was a rather strict isolationist, fellowshipping only with Southern Baptists, in which denomination I was converted, ordained, and partially educated. Things changed for me when I found that Spirit was thicker than blood.

Increasingly, ecumenism has become more of a conversation than a debate. This is not to obscure the dangers of a mind-emptying syncretism in order to merely get along. Christians may steadfastly uphold core doctrines and maintain distinctives without fear of contamination, and they find cooperating to meet human needs expands Christian witness.

Conversation Six

End Times

Eschatology is a big word and has to do with how one sees the last period of time for life on planet Earth. The relationship between the close of history and Christ's Second Coming poses several questions:
1. Will there be a millennium (i.e. an earthly reign of Jesus Christ)?
2. If so, will the Second Coming take place before or after that period?
3. Will Christ remove the church prior to a period of tribulation, or will He return and establish His kingdom only after that period?

I. Millennial Views

"Post," "Pre," and "A," millennial views have each been held by various groups and denominations of the church virtually throughout the entirety of church history. A more recent view (mid-nineteenth century) is Dispensationalism, somewhat similar to Premellenialism but with differences.

A.   **Postmillennialism : Christ returns after the millennium**

1. The advance of the gospel is so successful that the world is converted. The reign of Christ in human hearts will be universal and complete. Peace will prevail and evil will be banished.
2. A major tenet of Postmillennialism is the successful spread of the Gospel. It has been popular during periods in which the church appeared to be succeeding at its task of winning the world. The return of Christ occurs following a millennial period of a thousand years.

B.   **Premillennialism : Christ returns before the millennium**

1. Here Jesus returns, usually following a period of tribulation or persecution of the Church, and then reigns for a thousand years on earth.
2. After this earthly reign, the eternal kingdom of God begins in heaven.
3. This is arguably the historical position of the Church.

C.   **Amillennialism : Christ returns and there is no millennial period**

1. There will be no millennium – i.e., no thousand year earthly reign of Christ.
2. Despite Amillennialism's simplicity and the clarity of its central tenet, it is in many ways difficult to grasp. That is because its most notable feature is negative (no millennium), which overshadows its positive teachings.
3. Also, Amillennialists have trouble with Revelation 20:4-6, taking it symbolically (as did Augustine). They see the seven sections of the Book of Revelation as

recapitulations of the time period between Christ's first and second comings.

4. Further, they point out that nowhere else in Scripture is a one thousand year reign of Christ mentioned; rather it understands the thousand year millennium to be the time between the first and second advent.

D.   Dispensationalism: Christ returns following a rapture or taking up of the Church

1. There are considerable differences between Dispensationalists, but simply put—there is a rapture or taking up of the Church from the earth, some say secretly, others say "noisily."
2. Then a period of tribulation begins, either seven years or three and a half years long. Then there is a second, open and visible return of Jesus, and He sets up a thousand year reign from Jerusalem.
3. Israel will be converted in great numbers during the millennium. This is followed by a release of Satan in power for a short period, but he is destroyed by Jesus at a third return.
4. Dispensationalists put great emphasis on the covenant that God made with the nation of Israel as seen in the Old Testament. This is taken literally and not seen as prophetic material about the one People of God. Jesus will sit on David's throne and rule the world from Israel.
5. Non-Dispensationalists put less emphasis on national Israel, holding instead that Israel's special place will be found within the Church.

The rather hot debates over "what" and "how" and "when" of the end times has eased considerably among Christians. However, the fact of Christ's return remains a solid article of faith, as it should. The Old and New Testaments are clear about it, Jesus promised to return, and the Apostles' Creed says, "And he will come again to judge the living and the dead."

Presently, Postmillennialism has had some resurgence, but Premillennialism is still held by many. Amillennialism, arguably also having historic roots, is gaining in popularity. Dispensationalism, extremely popular for a century and more, is currently in decline.

The details of the Second Coming of Christ, a major interest for me as well as for countless other Christians, is now more of a conversation, and frequently is heard, "We will see how it all turns out."

What is held by all Christians is that Jesus will reign as Lord of lords and King of kings forever and ever with all the saints of all the ages, that there will be a great Day of Judgment, and that those whose names are not written in the Book of Life, along with the entire demonic kingdom, will be cast into hell forever and ever. Ultimately, Jesus and His Church win.

Conversation Seven

Gifts of the Holy Spirit

There are significant differences in the way Christians approach the subject of the charismatic gifts of the Holy Spirit.

It is generally agreed that upon conversion, which is the act of God in salvation, the Holy Spirit indwells each new Christian. It is the work of the Holy Spirit to apply the saving act of Jesus Christ to the individual by means of forgiveness of sin, placing that individual into the Body of Christ, which is the invisible Church. It is therefore the Holy Spirit who justifies, glorifies, sanctifies, and seals all those now in Christ.

A.   Lists of the Gifts in the New Testament

There are lists of charismatic or grace gifts that are given to born-again Christians found in Romans 12:6–8 and 1 Corinthians 12:4–11. There may be an additional gift mentioned in 1 Corinthians 7:6–7.

B.   Cessationism

Some argue that the charismatic gifts of the Holy Spirit disappeared or became unnecessary after the Apostolic Era and the publication of the New Testament. We use the word "cessationist" to identify this position.

Of course, there are variations on the theme. Some hold that only the so-called power gifts are no longer operative: miracles, speaking in tongues, healing, and maybe one or two others, while those like faith, contributing, leading, and some others are still active in the Church.

C. Continuationist

A second view is termed "continuationist," meaning that all of the gifts of the Holy Spirit continue to be in operation.

My own view straddles these two, and based mostly upon my own experience, I propose that the power gifts of the Holy Spirit may occasionally be in operation, especially during times of awakening and revival, while for most of the "normal" times they are not. Certainly this view makes for some rather lively discussion.

D. Baptism of the Holy Spirit

The Baptism of the Holy Spirit is another point of contention among Christians. John the Baptist said that one coming after him would baptize with the Holy Spirit and fire (see Matthew 3:11–12). Interpretations of this are quite varied. Some say this baptism does or should result in speaking in tongues. My own view is that the baptism of the Holy Spirit empowers us to be witnesses and preachers of the Gospel, and this comes from the very mouth of Jesus:

> So when they had come together, they asked him, "Lord, will you at this time restore the kingdom to Israel?" He said to them, "It is not for you to know times or seasons that the Father has fixed by his own authority. But you will receive power when the Holy Spirit has come upon you, and you will be my witnesses in Jerusalem, and

in all Judea and Samaria, and to the end of the earth." (Acts 1:6–8)

Regardless of what else is involved, Christians are to be filled or baptized with the Holy Spirit so they might be better equipped to present Jesus to a lost world.

Conversation Eight

Music in the Church

May we have music in church services? If so, voices only or also instruments? And if instruments, what limits must be placed? Do we allow organ or piano only, or may we add guitar, violin, or even a full-blown band with drums?

A. Biblical Citations

There are whole denominations that exclude music from weekly worship, using more or less valid proofs from Scripture: well, were there electric guitars twanging in the churches mentioned in the New Testament? Probably not, and not likely a drum set, organ, piano, or tambourine either (okay, maybe a tambourine).

There are musical instruments mentioned in the Old Testament—those used in temple worship as denoted in some of the Psalms. Instruments are not clearly mentioned in the New Testament, but there were "psalms, hymns, and spiritual songs" (see Ephesians 5:19 and Colossians 3:16).

Well then, is music in the church a debate or a conversation? My answer is conversation.

B.   The Purpose and Effects

What is really of concern here is not whether there should be music in the church but *how* music is used in the church. On this point a lot of noise is being made.

Does worship happen only when the band is playing? Is the time when eyes are closed, hands are in the air, and feet are doing the "Christian shuffle" the real worship?

According to some, the music is the real worship—not the call to worship, or the time of prayer and meditation, or when Scripture is read, or the offering taken, or the sermon preached, or the benediction given. No, only when the music carries a person to a place approaching a light trance state is there Holy Spirit-driven worship.

Perhaps the effects of music are not fully understood. Music can be deceiving, since it pushes the emotions out into the open, giving them sway over mental reasoning or even discerning the message of God in other parts of the service.

C.   What About Lyrics?

And it matters not what lyrics are being sung. The name of Jesus may be foremost and the words biblical in content, but this is not the point. Music has become center stage; in some venues taking over worship services to look more like an entertainment event than biblically oriented worship. An enthusiastic response to music, with visible and audible movin' and groovin' to the beat, has become the mark or indicator whether the Holy Spirit has "shown up" or not.

We old time rock and rollers may love to move and groove to the beat. For years I played in an actual band called Joyful Noise, and to this very day I lead a little praise band, playing the same guitar I did in 1968, belting out the old Jesus People songs. This, however, is a far cry from the way music can be used to manipulate emotions.

Is the Holy Spirit present in a feeling? Can the Holy Spirit drive or influence our emotions? Must we be emotionally stone cold in order to be biblically correct? My view is that no one knows the answers to these questions. Even now, at the closing of 2014, the Christian music scene is morphing, into what I am not sure, but it will change over time.

Conversation Nine

Origins

When and how did God create the universe? This question is variously answered by Bible-believing Christians and treated in thousands of books on the subject. Following is a brief survey of the ordinary options.

Some of us have a tendency to consign to the nether regions those who see things differently when it comes to interpreting Genesis. However, there are several understandings articulated in the broad Christian community as to when and how creation took shape. Much of this depends upon how one interprets the Bible, but all the views presented here are within the broad spectrum of possibilities that remain faithful to biblical categories, as I see them.

A.   Creationist

First, the classic creationist view posits a young earth, anywhere from 6,000 to 10,000 years old, with humans roaming the earth coexistent with dinosaurs. The centerpieces of this view are a literal creation in six actual twenty-four hour days, a real Garden of Eden, the first humans, Adam and Eve and their Fall into sin resulting in death, and a world-wide flood at the time of Noah. There is far more to it than this simple rendering, but this is its core.

B. Intelligent Design

Second, intelligent design or ID, and in the Christian version of it the Creator God constructs the vital elements of life. There are so many ways Christians and non-Christians look at ID, it becomes impossible to lay out all the options. A narrow and generalized account posits that all of observed life owes itself to a grand divine design. ID folks may accept an old or young earth and may accept a literalistic interpretation of the Genesis accounts of creation. Essentially, all DNA has been so programmed by God that even if Darwinism, i.e., natural selection with mutations, were operative, it is within the bounds of God's plan and moves only at the dictates of the Designer.

C. Theistic Evolution

Third, theistic evolution accepts whatever science says about origins. It holds to an old earth and an old universe created some 13.4 billion years ago, with a gradual development of life forms into what can be observed now. If all life on earth emanated from conditions found in a primordial soup that set the stage for the first molecule, then God originated that method in any case.

D. Combination of Views

Fourth is a view that combines elements of the first three. (As far as I know, this view has no title or other identification so far.) Here a literal creation of Adam and Eve is acknowledged without specifying periods of time. The Creator God established within DNA the capacity to adapt to whatever conditions in the environment humans would encounter, so ID is embraced, too. This allows for Darwinism, or more precisely neo-Darwinism, and for whatever science discovers along the way. This view accepts quibbling on just about everything, is aware there are mysteries galore, and is not overly concerned about details.

An ever increasing number of Christians these days enjoy discussions on origins, find them entertaining, even exciting, and don't worry about the orthodoxy of those who take a different tact.

This is a conversation and not a deal breaking debate.

Conversation Ten

Politics and War

Do Christians belong exclusively to a particular political party? No, of course not, but it must be acknowledged that many non-Christians think otherwise, particularly in America.

A.   On Politics

One may be politically conservative or liberal and still be a genuine born from above saved saint. These individuals can also share the common bond of the presence of the indwelling Holy Spirit and worship together in the same local congregation. Both the "staunch" conservative and the "progressive" liberal may be among God's elect! It would likely be a sign of a toxic or cultic nature to find a church that was clearly homogenous when it came to political affiliations.

And people change over time. Youth has a tendency to develop views that older people reject, and vice versa. It is almost like the motion of the pendulum that slowly swings from one extreme to the other. As the pace of life slows down, there tends to be a middle ground discovered that touches both left and right, embracing elements of each.

Christians living in different parts of the country or world will see life through the lens of their own experiences, and the dominant worldview or paradigm of their region will have a tremendous effect on their politics and interactions with government. Some will see government as protector, some as enemy. Those in a higher socio-economic class will identify differently than others. These tendencies are part of how it is to be human, including the effects of the Fall, sin, and the devil.

B.   On War

In regards to war, there are those who will fight for their country and there are those who will support their nation's cause but will not take up arms. The conscientious objector is well within the boundaries of living out his duty to God and fellow humans. And despite one's views of war, we all know that it is horrific and tragic and that Satan loves to see it destroy people's lives.

As to what constitutes a just war is open to debate; self-defense, whether personal or national, is usually accepted as a just reason to take up arms. Others completely disagree, pointing to Jesus' statement in the Sermon on the Mount about turning the other cheek. While each of us can acknowledge the wisdom of the admonishment to "strive for peace with everyone, and for the holiness without which no one will see the Lord" (Hebrews 12:14), it must be acknowledged that faithful Christians see things differently on the subject of national war and personal defense. It is a conversation, make no mistake, but it is certainly no real debate or argument.

Conversation Eleven

Reformed vs. Arminian Theologies

There are two basic theologies operative in Christianity today, both articulated four to five hundred years ago:

A. Reformed

Reformed theology emphasizes the acting of a sovereign God in conversion and sanctification, in which salvation is by faith alone in Christ alone. It acknowledges that all who are born from above (saved) had been thus determined before the foundation of the world. This view was once referred to as Pauline theology, then Augustinian theology, then Calvinism after the 16th century reformer John Calvin. Reformed is almost a synonym for Calvinism, but not quite.

B. Arminian

Arminian theology is named for the seventeenth century Dutch theologian, Jacobus Arminius, who emphasized the person's cooperation with God's provision for salvation in Christ in their conversion. The act of the human will in repentance and believing is necessary for salvation: God works and the sinner works, and salvation is the outcome. Grace is God's working in salvation; repenting and faith, though aided by the Holy Spirit, is something of which the individual is capable.

C. Personal Journey from Arminian to Reformed

In 1995 I moved from being a five-point Arminian, in the Charles Finney mold, to a two-point Calvinist. It is too long a story to recount here, but the short version is that I stumbled across the debate between Asahel Nettleton and Finney that took place during America's Second Great Awakening, roughly from 1798 to 1835. Nettleton said that if you provided means by which a person could become a Christian, i.e., through an altar call and/or the reciting of the "sinner's prayer," then there would be false conversions.[1] After twenty-nine years in professional ministry, coming to this understanding helped explain much of what I saw in my evangelistic focus. So I gradually moved toward a Reformed theology. I do not say "Calvinistic theology" any longer, since I have never studied any system, however biblically put together, that is not flawed in some way. At present, I will claim 4.5 points on the so-called Calvinistic scale.

My view is that God is sovereign, and it is strictly His good pleasure to call us who are dead in our trespasses and sins to His Son Jesus Christ through the working of His Holy Spirit. Perhaps Ephesians 2:4–5 says it all: "But God, being rich in mercy, because of the great love with which he loved us, even when we were dead in our trespasses, made us alive together with Christ—by grace you have been saved." And if that is not enough, then go to Romans 8:30: "And those whom he predestined he also called, and those whom he called he also justified, and those whom he justified he also glorified."

---

[1] Inviting people to make a public profession of faith in Jesus is perfectly biblical. The problem comes in affirming salvation on everyone who is baptized, joins a church, or repeats the sinner's prayer.

When I first encountered Reformed Theology it made me angry. It was beyond both my understanding (and pride?) that the human will could be by-passed. After a while I calmed down and things went from being a hot debate to a conversation. In recent years, really from about 2000 to the present, the rise of the "new Calvinists" has brought the whole issue to a point of division between people choosing sides, sticking to their positions, and digging in.

The Miller Avenue Baptist Church of which I am pastor has an assortment of people of differing theologies, and we freely debate our positions. Guest preachers range from staunch dispensationalist Arminiams to "ten" point Calvinists and everything in between. Our fellowship is built around Jesus and not on theological systems. I present my own take on Reformed theology from time to time, but I am not insistent on conformity and instead invite discussion.

Our sovereign God, who has things firmly in control regardless of our methodologies or theologies, works for His good pleasure to save those whom He has predetermined for salvation in the time, place, and manner that He chooses.

So conversation is where I put this one.

Conversation Twelve

Women in the Church

In this topic, the operative or fighting words are "egalitarian" and "complementarian." From my limited perspective we are talking about a conversation, but it could move to an argument. And how sad that would be.

Very briefly, egalitarian is the idea that men and women are equal in their roles in the ministry of the church, whereas complementarian is the idea that a woman's God-given role is to support the work of men in the church.

A.   Complementarian

Complementarians base their position mostly on verses from Paul's writings: 1 Timothy 2:9–15 and 1 Corinthians 14:34. In the first passage, Paul wrote, "I do not permit a woman to teach or to exercise authority over a man; rather, she is to remain quiet" (1 Timothy 2:12). In the second we find, "The women should keep silent in the churches. For they are not permitted to speak, but should be in submission, as the Law also says" (1 Corinthians 14:34).

B. Egalitarian

It may appear that the above passages say it all, but the egalitarian argues that Paul is merely responding to specific situations in churches where certain behavior needed to be curtailed. A further argument points to other Scriptures that balance the scales. Appeal may be made to the prophet Joel, speaking about the Pentecostal outpouring of the Spirit, who declares that the Spirit will be poured out on all flesh; "your sons and your daughters shall prophesy" and "even on the male and female servants in those days I will pour out my Spirit" (Joel 2:28–29). Next comes Galatians 3:28: "There is neither Jew nor Greek, there is neither slave nor free, there is neither male nor female, for you are all one in Christ Jesus."

Besides the foregoing there are passages in the New Testament where it appears that women were directly involved in church ministry, especially alongside Paul himself. Among these are Acts 18:26; Romans 16:1, 3, 6, 7, 12, and 15. How unnatural it would be if these women did not impact a man or two.

In my four-plus decades of pastoral ministry, I have seen many dozens of women live out their spiritual gifts in churches, and men were naturally touched by these. Many churches in the developing world must rely on the services of women pastors, since the men must work full time just to put food on the table. It is difficult to imagine the exercise of a spiritual gift without words, whether spoken or written. Additionally, I have seen more men than women bring chaos and division to local churches.

It has been suggested that in some of the churches Paul knew of, the new found freedom of Roman women had spilled over into the church. Perhaps the new freedom found in Christ and the receiving of spiritual gifts was problematic for both men and women. No one, it seems, can be sure of how this should be understood.

Those of us who land mostly on the side of the egalitarians may receive the "slippery slope" accusation. This indictment may be little more than a disingenuous form of intimidation, yet historically, in certain instances, it is a valid consideration.

Compared with the four major debates expressed in part one of this second section, the role of women in the church will not likely reach the same status. It will hopefully remain a conversation.

Final Note

The four debates are lines drawn in the sand or chiseled in stone— incontrovertible. Here we take our stand.

The Church has vigorously stood for its revealed truths as part of its evangelical worldwide ministry from its inception and will do so right up to its completion.

The Church will be purified as the kernel is separated from the chaff, especially as regarding the major debates (see 1 John 2:19 and 1 Corinthians 11:19). This has long gone on, usually due to persecution, the presence of heretical movements, and the need to fulfill the commandment to take the Gospel to all the nations. Strength comes out of struggle, and that which is really the Church grows stronger.

The twelve conversations, however, pose the greater threat, unless Christians practice the policy of agreeing to disagree. It is not always simple or clear to arrive at what is clearly Scriptural; often we lose both perspective and humility, both of which should characterize followers of Jesus.

Other Books by Kent Philpott

The Soul Journey: How Shamanism, Santería, Wicca, and Charisma are Connected

If the Devil Wrote a Bible (Vols. 1 & 2)

Memoirs of a Jesus Freak

Awakenings in America and the Jesus People Movement

Deliver Us from Evil: How Jesus Casts Out Demons Today

A Matter of Life and Death: Understanding True and False Conversion

Are You Being Duped?

Why I Am a Christian (Vols. 1 & 2)

For Pastors of Small Churches

How to Care for Your Pastor

EVP

Available at: www.evpbooks.com

www.ingramcontent.com/pod-product-compliance
Lightning Source LLC
Chambersburg PA
CBHW022116040426
42450CB00006B/727